READY TO DIE!

DATE DUE

THE LIFE AND TIMES

of

BIGGIE SMALLS

THE NOTORIOUS B.I.G.

A BRILLIANT ARTIST!

—Vibe magazine

LEGENDARY TALENT!

—The Source

A TRUE GENIUS!

—Rolling Stone

NOTORIOUS B.I.G. (CHRISTOPHER WALLACE) QUICKLY BECAME A HOUSEHOLD NAME AMONG HIP-HOP FANS, AND ALL RESPONSIBILITY WOULD REST ON HIM AS HE MADE HIS WAY UP HIP-HOP'S AISLES TO CENTER STAGE. WHAT TOOK HIP-HOP BY STORM WITH THE DEBUT OF NOTORIOUS B.I.G. WAS HIS CANDID RAPPING STYLE, WHICH OPERATED MUCH IN THE SPIRIT OF THE DRUG TRADE HE HAD COME UP IN. HE SEEMED TO WELCOME THE CHALLENGE, AS HE WAS ALREADY RESIGNED TO HIS FATE, HENCE, READY FOR DEATH, OR WHATEVER THE WORLD COULD THROW AT HIM.

AUTHOR JAKE BROWN EXPLOSIVELY WRITES WHY IT WAS HIS TIME. HE DIDN'T LIVE IN OR UP TO THE MOMENT…HE CREATED IT.

BIGGIE CONTROLLED HIS TIME, BY THE VERY NATURE OF WHAT HE ACHIEVED IN IT. AND WHEN HIS TIME WAS UP, HE HAD DONE WHAT HE SET OUT TO DO

…AND IT WAS HISTORIC

READY TO DIE

THE STORY OF BIGGIE SMALLS

NOTORIOUS B.I.G.

King of the World & New York City

**Fast Money, Puff Daddy, Faith and Life After Death
The Unauthorized Biography**

Jake Brown

Colossus Books

Phoenix

New York   Los Angeles

First Edition
READY TO DIE: THE STORY OF BIGGIE SMALLS
NOTORIOUS B.I.G.
King of the World & New York City
Fast Money, Puff Daddy, Faith and Life After Death: The Unauthorized Biography

by Jake Brown

Published by:
Colossus Books
A Division of Amber Communications Group, Inc.
1334 East Chandler Boulevard, Suite 5-D67
Phoenix, Z 85048
amberbk@aol.com
WWW.AMBERBOOKS.COM

Tony Rose, Publisher/Editorial Director	Samuel P. Peabody, Associate Publisher
Yvonne Rose, Senior Editor	Namik Minter, Cover Design
The Printed Page, Interior Design	Interior Photos by Walik Gorshorn

Library of Congress Cataloging-in-Publication Data

Brown, Jake.
   Ready to die : the story of Biggie Smalls, Notorious B.I.G. King of the world & New York City : fast money, Puff Daddy, faith and life after death : the unauthorized biography / by Jake Brown.
      p. cm.
   Includes bibliographical references (p.).
   ISBN 0-9749779-3-4
      1. Notorious B.I.G. (Musician) 2. Rap musicians--United States--Biographies. I. Title.

ML420.N76B76   2004
782.421649'092--dc22
[B]

2004047760

Dedicated to Alexandra Federov,
the *BIG*gest fan of the Notorious one I know,
and one of the dearest friends I have…

Contents

Author's Notes

As a life-long hip-hop fan of both the East and West Coast, I grew up listening to rap without any allegiance other than to the music. I was amused by the lyrical beefs between 1980s rap superstars like Big Daddy Kane and Ice T with their counterpart LL Cool J, who, at his worst, threatened to "squash you like a Jelly Bean."

As that was my childhood, it was also coincidently hip-hop's, wherein rap as a commercial entity was only a few years old, and still evolving. By that fact, much of the content of hip-hop's broader message was innocent—most often about groupies—break dancing, riches, partying, driving expensive cars.

There was competition among hip-hop peers, but it was purely competitive as everyone was still on the come-up. In a comparative sense to the state of hip-hop a few years later on, in the early 1990s, the aforementioned content was at best peripheral—wherein references were made to the violence and poverty that ravaged inner-city America and its populous, but rarely explicitly—at least not without Tipper Gore's dreaded 'Parental Advisory Sticker', which all but banished an artist's album from mainstream exposure in the days of Run DMC and Kool Moe Dee.

All that changed as hip-hop became a teenager and began rebelling, wherein 'gangster rap' artists like N.W.A. and Ice T came to popularity, selling platinum albums with almost no radio play or video support on MTV.

Opening the doors for Death Row Records' takeover in 1992, the exposure became even greater for rap fans as Dr. Dre and Suge Knights' arsenal of gangland-affiliated rap stars like Snoop Doggy Dogg rapped candidly over hooky, top-40 friendly instrumentals about their gang affiliations, drug dealing, arrests and prison time, and run-ins with fellow gangs.

The graphic nature of the lyrical content of this music, for example concerning the open discussion of automatic weapons like the AK-47 Assault Rifle and the 9 Millimeter or Glock hand guns, had previously been only as focused on by pop culture in the context of action movies starring Sylvester Stallone and Arnold Schwartzenegger.

As the decade wore on, and both Tupac Shakur and the Notorious B.I.G. brought hip-hop full circle as a billion-dollar, mainstream entity unto itself, the violence and sexual content that hip-hop artists requisitely and regularly displayed in their music stood in stark contrast, almost as a stranger, to the memory I had as a young listener of rap as a fledgling sound not ten years earlier. I had grown into a teenager myself, so of course I accepted and embraced the evolution of hip-hop, specifically its lyrical content, as a reflection of reality, which in many cases, it was.

Looking back in a historical sense, I like to compare hip-hop's evolution and inherent change in both lyrical and visual content to that of Hollywood's own evolution over the years from the infancy of black and white, silent films in the 1920s and 1930s to the revolution of color film, sound, and special effects. A movie like Rambo would have been banned in the 1930s, but as the film medium advanced through the next 60 years as our most popular and diversified storytelling medium, movies themselves became reflections of life and reality around us.

The same has been true for hip-hop in its short 30-year history. The evolution itself was much more rapid, but it was conceptually identical in terms of the listening public's desensitization where the increasingly graphic nature of the content—both lyrically and visually—was concerned over the course of the late 1980s and 1990s.

In today's age, it's as common to expect to hear about a violent murder in a rap song, as it is to watch one on a movie screen. However, just as a popular movie star can play a killer, he can also turn around and play a romantic lead in the very next movie. The same 180-degree topical transition is expected in rap, and considered as common and accepted among hip-hop artists. Where one single a rapper is talking about participating in gang violence, on the next song he is rapping about being the consummate lover of the ladies—in the case of Biggie Smalls, Gimmie the Loot vs. Big Poppa.

And while the violence in hip-hop lyrics are often a reflection of the environment their orators grew up in and around, often rappers will concede to some degree that they are playing out a persona, representing friends, or the spirit of their larger neighborhood through a character in a song, rather than actually having walked every line they talk.

Both Biggie Smalls and Tupac fell into the latter category at times throughout their respective careers—where some of what they rapped about they may have experienced. For instance, Biggie hustling crack…but it is highly unlikely that Wallace ever personally murdered anyone, as he often rapped about in the course of his rhymes. He did so as convincingly as an actor, because in a very real sense, he was in fact playing a role.

The same was true with Tupac, who most that knew him feel he began to act out the gangster persona of his character Bishop in the Eric Dickerson movie Juice, following the movie's release and subsequent success. While Shakur was more of an on-the-job trainee in terms of earning his stripes as a real criminal, the public bought the persona—lock, stock and barrel.

Off screen and off record, Tupac and Biggie were both young men, in their early 20s respectively, both looking to make it to the big time. In the course of their rise, they would help one another out, become friends, united, and then suddenly divided as quickly as they had come together by a tragic robbery-shooting that came dangerously close to claiming Shakur's life.

Unfortunately, a personal misunderstanding between Smalls and Shakur would become a business opportunity for many, who had nothing privately vested in the dispute, and whose only true motive was the pursuit of money and power over any real interest in peace. The media played a prominent role as catalyst for blowing the conflict so out of control that it would ultimately cost both Shakur and Smalls their lives. I am not sure that their loss to the hip-hop nation can ever be compensated, and certainly not out of the billions of dollars the press and corporate record labels made at the expense of these young men's lives. That money is truly blood money.

The dispute did not concern the media, nor the rest of the country, nor hip-hop as a larger entity; but soon it would consume all of us, myself included. In the end, the East Coast/West Coast beef was sadly no more than a fad, a phase, another turn in hip-hop's revolution, but it was a revolution—because both of these men were prophetic in the end, in their message, influence upon the industry, and iconic status in its history books.

To acknowledge the tragedy in any positive sense is perhaps to view it as a tragedy that cannot ever again repeat itself, by the very nature of its major players, and the fact that their respective individual talents and broader contributions to the game cannot ever again be repeated.

As young as hip-hop is as an entity, Tupac Shakur and the Notorious B.I.G. will be viewed 50 years from now—when hip-hop is 80+ years old—as forefathers. They had, and continue to have, no contemporaries; and I have been equally as influenced as a listener by both of them. I think inevitably we all have. More importantly, we don't want our heroes to die, and so we continue to keep them alive through our purchase of their existing catalog, as well as of the volumes of previously unreleased material that continues to emerge from both rappers' archives.

The purchase of this music is a true celebration of both rappers' legacies, as the releases are authorized through the estates of both Shakur and Wallace, and whose heirs most benefit from the sales, rather than the news media or corporate scum f**ks whose only interest would be in exploiting the memory of either rapper for their own gain.

In the literary and cinematic mediums, there have been volumes of material released on both Tupac Shakur and the Notorious B.I.G. in the years following their respective murders, and most of it has been as sensational in content as the very media blitz that first drove the East Coast/West Coast beef to the tragic end it suffered. Comedians like Chris Rock have joked that society cannot blame the media for black on black crime.

Sadly, however, in reality, it is the wider public perceptions created, planted and harvested by the media of the young black male that have been, at least in part, responsible for the biases and limited expectations that many sects of society attach to their stereotype for the inner city African American male. The news media is as much an exercise in making money as it is in free speech, and the latter is more often than not used as a front for the former.

The national attention paid to the East Coast/West Coast beef was no different in terms of the biased nature of the coverage toward the end of selling more papers and magazines by enflaming the conflict to make it larger in nature than it truly was. When Sean Combs, or Suge Knight, or Tupac, or Biggie would shoot down the suggestion that there was an East Coast/West Coast beef, any number of hip-hop or general media journalists would rephrase the same question, and pound the aforementioned parties with it until they got some remotely useful sound-bite. If they got silence, the reporter would find a way to exploit that too, suggesting fear on the part of the silent party (usually Combs and Wallace), invariably forcing them to respond or risk looking or sounding soft to their audience.

Where it could be argued that Suge Knight and Tupac Shakur hold some of the blame for recognizing the media attention as an opportunity to sell records, Wallace and Combs remained largely diplomatic throughout the majority of the conflict, routinely making calls for peace.

In that spirit, this book is the first of its kind with respect to the life and times of Christopher Wallace, in that its focus is on just that—*his life and times*—not his death. Nor who might be responsible, nor in the absence of legitimate suspects, who the media decides to name as the guilty parties, nor the conspiracy the press has suggested exists around why both men's deaths remain unsolved.

We solve nothing by continuing to contribute to the media-created riddle surrounding Biggie and Tupac's murders. In both cases, thus far, where there is smoke, there HAS NOT BEEN FIRE. Only speculation, exploitation, conjecture, and a concentrated attempt to continue to fan a flame that died down years ago for most true hip-hop fans. This book is for you, and I hope through reading it you gain a better understanding of the life and times of Christopher Wallace as a person, an MC, a father, a son, a friend, a visionary, and an Icon.

Many considered Biggie ahead of his time, I think he was his time. He didn't live in or up to the moment ...he created it. He controlled his time, by the very nature of what he achieved in it. And when his time was up, he had done what he set out to do, and it was historic.

I believe that while Biggie had even bigger plans, he would look back upon his professional legacy, with no regrets. I hope you, as the reader, do not close this book with any of your own, and hope you enjoy what I believe to be the first real look at the life and times of Biggie Smalls, what really made him the Notorious BIG, and ultimately, the King of New York!

—Jake Brown

Introduction

By the time Christopher Wallace, aka Notorious B.I.G. aka Biggie Smalls' chapter came to be written in hip-hop's history book, the genre's roots had already become gentrified, wherein the concept of the ghetto experience was a hallmark among suburban record buyers throughout America's midsection.

In fact, most hip-hop fans and critics have agreed that by mid-1994, when Bad Boy Entertainment dropped the debut LP by Notorious B.I.G., hip-hop's belly was a little overstuffed with the concept of gangster rap. Public Enemy, at their pinnacle the equivalent of hip-hop's Malcom X, had taken the concept of black power and its inherent struggle to peak within the pop culture, via protest anthems like *Fight the Power* and *Bring the Noise*.

Fellow hip-hop artists such as MC Hammer and Kid N Play had taken advantage of the genre's popularity among the white record buying mainstream by creating a corporate-friendly image that resonated principally with major television networks who designed Saturday morning cartoons around both of them.

Advertisers such as Kentucky Fried Chicken featured MC Hammer in a series of television commercials. N.W.A. founder, Ice Cube, had summarized hip-hop's faltering edginess in his 1992 hit single *True to the Game*, attacking Hip-hop's 'sell out' faction as what had watered down hard core rap to the point where it had begun to lose its potency, charging "then ya crossed over, on MTV, but they don't care, they'll have a new nigga next year…and ya might have a heart attack, when ya find out the black folks don't want ya back".

When Notorious B.I.G. dropped his aptly titled debut LP, *Ready to Die*, it became more than a personal statement for the artist himself, as hip-hop fans across the nation embraced the album as a broader-ranging statement of what hip-hop had lost, and a prophecy for what it ultimately risked losing if the genre, as a whole, didn't reconnect with its urban roots.

Hip-hop was bloated, but would soon be appropriately deflated with the potent dose of reality that *Ready to Die* would provide. The album's powerful combination of pure reality rhymed over dance friendly beats rooted principally in the vein of 1970's R&B making it stand out above the rest. The effect, at first, came off like *Soul Hits Volume 13*, stripped of its vocal tracks, and replaced with Biggie Smalls' rapping. It was the freshest form of plagiarism that hip-hop's sample-friendly culture had experienced in ages.

While Biggie Smalls himself had protested the pop-friendly orientation of the album's backing tracks, particularly the Puffy-produced singles like *Big Poppa* and *One More Chance*, even B.I.G. couldn't deny the potency of the formula's mix. Biggie's realism served up to hungry listeners on a top-40 radio friendly platter, providing immediate crossover potential.

While many rap critics argued that Sean Puffy Combs hadn't helped the goal of toning down hip-hop's already inflated sound with *Ready to Die's* production, which some thought was as glossy as the suits Puffy often pranced around in throughout the background of his artists' videos, Biggie Smalls' authenticity was ultimately undeniable. As for Smalls himself, he didn't care what his critics thought, as long as his sound resonated with hip-hops record buyers, and the money was rolling in.

By the time *Juicy* had blown up on hip-hop radio, Notorious B.I.G. was quickly becoming a household name among hip-hop fans, and in the same time providing East Coast's rap scene with exactly the boost it needed in sales to once again become a bona fide player among hip-hop's elite. All responsibility rested on Notorious B.I.G. as he made his way up hip-hop's aisles to center stage. He seemed to welcome the challenge, as he was already resigned to his fate, hence, ready for death, or whatever the world could throw at him.

Part of Biggie's edge was throwing off his critics with songs like *Ready to Die* and *Suicidal Thoughts*, which touched on subject matter too legitimate to deny or brush aside with a criticism concerning a beat or the way a loop was sampled repeatedly. Perhaps that was part of Biggie's strategy, but as he explained it, the subject of death was very much a part of his mentality, based on the reality that engulfed him: "The situation was where I had the gun to my head and was thinking it over because I was tired of being in the mind state of having to hustle just to feed my daughter at the time. And just being in that mind state selling drugs and just being in the street 'cause my mother told me to get out her house. Everything was just looking real down. I was to the point where if I did kill myself, nobody would miss me. That was the ideal behind *Suicidal Thoughts*."

Above and beyond how *Ready to Die* applied individually to Biggie's reality, his debut served as a shank in the spine of the cheesy over-commercialized elements that had smoothed their way into rap's middle class record buying populous like a fast talking vacuum salesman might have. Hard core hip-hop fans were no longer buying the fast food corniness that New Jack was selling. As a Rolling Stone Critic raved near the end of his review of B.I.G.'s debut, *Ready to Die* is the strongest hip-hop debut since Ice Cube's *Amerikkka's Most Wanted*.

Hip-hop artists have traditionally revered Al Pacino's character in the classic 1981 narcotics flick *Scarface*, in their rhymes as a role model for the status they aimed to achieve, as street hustlers in the drug sport of selling crack cocaine. An all too common theme in hop-hop, narcotics have proven to be the most lucrative job prospect for many African American males in the inner city's projects and ghetto neighborhoods in the past forty years. With limited legitimate earning prospects, the flash of the narcotics trade found a home in America's streets.

As the street drug trade followed a hierarchy, with foot soldiers selling bigger dealers' product for a smaller share of the profit, the trickle down connection between the immediate gratification of fast cash, and any implied longevity within the upper ranks of the narcotics game were far apart from one another.

The crack game, by design, kept street hustlers just enough ahead of the legitimate game to justify their continuing to do it, based on the prospect of rising in the ranks. Such a decision was a common sense choice in many cases when faced with the alternatives, i.e. a $4.50 an hour job at McDonalds. The negative effects this trade had on America's inner cities were, in the long run, devastating.

Gang violence waged over corner spots where product was sold, addiction ran rampant through inner city households, often where (utilized as a coping device for the impoverished reality) many African Americans were forced to reside.

Ultimately the numbers of street hustlers who did get caught up in the legal system as a result of their involvement with the narcotics trade raised the prison population nearly five times over from the beginning of the 1980s through the 1990s. "The number of drug offenders handled by state and federal prisons rose by 510% from 1983 to 1993, to 353,564 people from 57,975".

This was Biggie Smalls' reality between the ages of 17, when he was kicked out of his mother's house for selling drugs to support his daughter, and 21, when he would first catch the ear of future Bad Boy CEO, Sean Puffy Combs at Uptown Entertainment.

Combs signed Biggie to a development deal before taking the rapper along when he left to form his own label.

This shot would almost be missed by a nine-month prison stint Biggie picked up selling narcotics in North Carolina, and a near-bust that would have landed him in state prison: "It's a part of the daily struggle, man. If you coming outside with jacks in your pockets, and you call yourself hustlin', you got to be ready for a lot of things. You got to be ready for the stick-up man and for the police. Niggas that slip up get bagged, that's just something they got to handle. Ain't nobody gonna put crack in they hand and say, 'I'm not getting locked up, I'm not going to jail.' I had that ready for me, you know what I'm sayin'? It just happened. I just maintained and handled my business, and I'm home. Stressed, but I'm home.'"

The first legitimate advocate, or voice of reason, for America's drug-saddled inner-city generation came via hip-hop. It arrived by the late 1980s, notably with the debut of 'reality rap' which documented the upsides and downsides of life in the drug ridden ghetto neighborhoods and via old school classics like N.W.A.'s *Straight Outta Compton*, which provided a harrowing illustration of life in the gangland neighborhood in South Central Los Angeles.

This trend caught on like wildfire, captivating a nation of largely white, suburban teenage listeners, who up until that point, had been restricted to television shows like *Miami Vice* and movies like *Scarface* for the exposure to the perils of the inner cities. Hip-hop gave them an identity, with which to contrast the boredom that was inherent in the safety of the suburbs.

As the trend of reality rap moved East, so too did the first true boom of hip-hop sales in the very early part of the 1990s, led by Suge Knight and Dr. Dre's Death Row Records, which did $60 million in sales as an independent label its first year in business with the success of Dr. Dre's *The Chronic*.

Where East Coast rap had held the edge in the early and mid 1980's with the success of powerhouse groups like Run DMC, Public Enemy, and Eric B and Rakim, the West Coast had taken over the show with the debut of N.W.A. Such that, by the beginning of 1993, East Coast hip-hop needed a new heavyweight to retake the championship belt that New York had lost to Los Angeles.

Despite this inequity, there were still plenty of wanna-be contenders winning notable bouts for hip-hop's cause, principally on MTV and the Billboard top 200, where more and more rap acts were beginning to cross over from the second class R&B charts to share in the wealth of mainstream acceptance.

Back on the corners of America's inner cities, the effect of hip-hop's mainstream crossover was being felt among millions of young African American males, who had begun to pair the prospect of succeeding in hip-hop, alongside making it as a pro athlete, as an alternative to the narcotics avenue and as a means of rising above the perils of the inner city. Even if only a concept for 98% of those who dreamt of escaping poverty to superstardom, whether it be in the Bedford Stuyvesant section of Brooklyn, New York, or in South Central Los Angeles, the generic affect was the same.

As one of the aforementioned, an up and coming hip-hop MC and crack dealer named Christopher Wallace, who went by the aliases Biggie Smalls, and Notorious B.I.G., would later characterize it on his debut LP, "If I wasn't in the rap game, I'd probably have a key, Knee deep in the crack game, because the streets is a short stop, either you slanging crack rock, or you got a wicked jump shot."

What took hip-hop by storm with the debut of Notorious B.I.G. was his candid rapping style, which, operating much in the spirit of the drug trade he had come up in, took no shorts. This was primarily ensured by the fact that Biggie Smalls and executive producer Sean "Puffy" Combs had spent almost two years making

Ready To Die, and the finished product was a perfectly rounded experience for any hip-hop listener. It covered all spectrums of the hustler psyche; from the ups of instant money, notoriety, and constant female and fan adulation to the downs of the stress that accompanies becoming an overnight sensation.

And, the real life stakes, in Biggie's case, included his mother's breast cancer, the birth of his daughter, and his own clinically diagnosed depression. He was a human being beneath the shades of sensationalism. Biggie Smalls was hip-hop's first openly vulnerable MC, and his trump card was laying his hand on the table, putting everything on the line.

In doing so, he provided a platter of subject matter broad enough for everyone to eat off of: "(My album's) just like a big pie, with each slice indicating a different point in my life involving bitches, niggas…from the beginning to the end. I feel I made an East Coast movie, for niggas on both sides to recognize and respect. I'm trying to do everything. I got party records, songs for ladies, stories. I just didn't want to leave it one way, 'cause I think that's a problem to me, because if I rap a certain way I'm only gonna get money that one certain way. If everybody rapped about different things that other people can relate to, then you can get other money. It's all about money, man. You a fool if you [say] 'I'm in it for the love of Hip-Hop!' you in it for the cream, straight up and down, baby bro. 'Cause hip-Hop ain't gonna pay that car note. Hip-hop is not gonna pay the rent. The money is…I was like… ready to do whatever I had to do to get dough. Even if it involved risking my life, I just had to make it happen."

The debut of *Ready To Die* made Notorious B.I.G. an overnight sensation, but he seemed to handle the transition too naturally, possibly because he came off as the first hungry MC to take a seat at hip-hop's table in a long while. What made his authenticity stand out above and beyond other up-and-coming rap artists was the fact that his feet were still firmly rooted on the block, making it seem as though he had just changed occupations, rather than anything fundamental in terms of his lifestyle.

This honesty, in hip-hop terms, meant Biggie Smalls kept it constantly real:"Growin' up in the streets of Bed-Stuy was hard yo. I mean, either you was stealin', or you was hustling…one of the two…or you wasn't nobody; or you was playin' ball, wantin' to be some college pro type. It was hard. Everybody was scramblin', everybody still scramblin'…ain't nothing changed. The transition from selling drugs to the game was like…it was strong…it was like, I was a hustler, then, boom, I was a rapper. So…like, when I was in the hood, and I was hustling, and a car pull up…staring, I would probably grip up on my joint…not knowin' what's the deal. But now me being a rapper, that same car pull up, it could be a fan, you know, they could want an autograph. It's kind of shaky, but its cool…if I Wasn't rapping, I'd probably be hustling to get money to take care of my family. "

The next four years of Biggie Smalls' life would be lived in the fast lane—with a marriage to R&B singer Faith Evans that followed a twelve day courtship; the birth of two children…a boy and a girl; a romance with protégé Lil Kim that would result in an aborted child and cruel tabloid headlines; the rise of Bad Boy Entertainment, which would make Sean Puffy Combs a mogul in his own right, and pave the way for Biggie's crew, The Junior Mafia; and a series of criminal arrests for offenses ranging from assault to robbery to weapons and narcotic possession.

As Biggie's success jumpstarted East Coast hip-hop's stalled engine, it started in the same time a media-fueled bi-coastal beef between East Coast Bad Boy Records and West Coast Death Row Records, rooted in a personal difference between the respective coast's two biggest stars, LA's Tupac Shakur, and NY's B.I.G., that would ultimately cost both rappers their lives.

Biggie Smalls' rhymes dealt with the reality of violence head on, and like most hip-hop artists who fell within the gangsta rap niche of the genre, he had his own philosophy for why violence was so integrally woven into rap's collective fabric. In Biggie's eyes, it clearly went beyond a matter of the stuff that sells platinum records. Possibly, this was because he lived a more authentic variation of what, in many cases, were popularly referred to as studio gangsters, who rapped about a violent lifestyle in generic terms because they had limited experience with its realities in the course of their own.

While most hip-hop fans and critics alike felt Biggie sidekick Sean Puffy Combs unequivocally fell into the latter category, Notorious B.I.G. himself came off with the opposite impression. Biggie could never fabricate the reality of his background, as hip-hop was in a way his therapy: "This gansta-rap shit. It's like, they're making mountains out of molehills. I figure like this. You could take a Black person off the streets. Take him away from the drugs and crime. Give him money to sing about stuff that he's been through. Regardless of the fact of what it is, you should never stop him from doing that. You change his lifestyle. Completely cut the ghetto and put him under a bunch of business mothafuckas, just for what he can say. And after he does it, they have no right to analyze it. These people never lived in buildings like this-AK shots just gettin' rang off. They've never been there, so they have no right to say 'This is too harsh.'"

Biggie's rhymes hit hip-hop listeners in their collective gut. Especially within the boroughs of New York, *Ready to Die* was a soundtrack for life within the street culture of Queens, Brooklyn, Manhattan, and the Bronx. Whether you drove down Atlantic Boulevard in Brooklyn, or Queens Boulevard, or through Harlem, looking around, Biggie's lyrical imagery represented the many moods of New York's streets.

Whether the energy of the hungry hustler, or the instability of poverty, or the paranoia that the random violence within the projects invoked, the general frustrations that accompany being a young, black male in America, or chilling with a crew of friends on an apartment building vestibule in Brooklyn, the same current of authenticity ran through the experience of each listener.

Biggie Smalls was preaching the word of the everyday struggle, and his message was universal while at the same time personal to every ear that he had listening. He represented on record for his city like a congressman might, except Biggie's constituents were the hustlers like those in his Junior Mafia crew. The faceless crack addicts like the ones he sold to before blowing up in the rap game, the single mothers like his own who were stuck raising a generation of father-less young black males …all the ranks of the lower class who had no real voice speaking for them before *Ready to Die* hit the charts.

In the centerpiece of his campaign on *Ready to Die*, the most direct indictments of those elements of society that worked to keep the lower African American classes systematically oppressed were captured in the albums most poignant pair of songs, *Juicy* and *Everyday Struggle*, wherein Biggie Smalls breaks it down with a chilling accuracy and honesty that most politicians could never be capable of.

"I'm seeing body after body and our mayor Guiliani, ain't tryin to see no black man turn to John Gotti…Dealin with the dope fiend binges, seein syringes in the veins, hard to explain, how I maintain, the crack smoke make my brain feel so strange…I know how it feel to wake up fucked up, Pockets broke as hell, another rock to sell, People look at you like you use the user, Selling drugs to all the losers, mad buddha abuser, But they don't know about your stress-filled day, Baby on the way mad bills to pay, That's why you drink Tangueray, so you can reminisce, and wish, you wasn't livin so devilish."

Biggie never sought to deny anything in his indictment of both himself and the system's role in putting him in that position. Above and beyond any ulterior motives, he sought to unapologetically represent the reality around him, partly because he knew it was the avenue to making the most money. Biggie, as a hustler, knew his role, and in applying that mentality to the hip-hop game, was unstoppable. It was a bottom line reality that even his mother had to accept: "My moms don't like my music, she thinks I got the filthiest mouth in the world, but she understands that I'm doing this because she knows I'm about to get paid; my daughter's going to be set, and I'm gonna get her that house in Florida that she wants. She knows this. I mean, how could I not? what else do I know?"

In the final analysis, Biggie Smalls shared a similar affinity for his city that his cinematic idol, drug lord Frank White, played chillingly by Christopher Walkin, had in Albert Ferrera's 1990 classic *King of New York*. Where most rappers generically aligned themselves with Al Pacino's Tony Montana in *Scarface*, Biggie Smalls had an edge with Frank White that few MCs would have been clever enough to lay claim to.

The title was now literally Biggie's, and as he blew up with his debut release, the press and fans alike, along with fellow hip-hop MCs on both coasts, were forced to recognize Biggie's status as Frank White's namesake, *The King of New York*. In short, no one could touch his ambition. He translated that drive into whatever the necessary medium was to escape his impoverished childhood: "Put the drugs on the shelf? Nah, couldn't see it, *Scarface, King of New York*, I wanna be it...Tremendous cream, fuck a dollar and a dream...Still tote gats strapped with infrared beams."

The release of *Ready to Die* was a new dawn for Biggie Smalls, and though fate would ultimately call his bluff, that dark prophecy's truth would escape him for four glorious and notorious years to come, during which Biggie Smalls would not only become the *King of New York*, but one of the pre-eminent hip-hop icons of the 1990s.

—Jake Brown

Now I'm thirteen, smokin' blunts, makin' cream
On the drug scene, fuck a football team
Riskin' ruptured spleens by the age of sixteen
Hearin' the coach scream ain't my lifetime dream, I mean
I wanna blow up, stack my dough up
So school I didn't show up, it fucked my flow up…

Rap was secondary, money was necessary
Until I got incarcerated—kinda scary
C74-Mark 8 set me straight
Not able to move behind the great steel gate
Time to contemplate, damn, where did I fail?
All the money I stacked was all the money for bail

—Biggie Smalls, *Respect*, 1994

Chapter 1
The Man vs. The Myth

What is the hardest thing one could say about the Notorious B.I.G.? What if by *hardest*, we weren't referring to the gangster exterior of Biggie's image? What if *hardest* means most *difficult*, or that which *challenged* us most about the inherent and fairly obvious contradictions that existed within Christopher Wallace's true involvement within the everyday struggle he rapped so eloquently and vividly about?

It's easy to believe the hard times Biggie rapped about because they have historically been so commonplace in the ghetto. However, when one truly examines Biggie's childhood as it happened, according to loved ones, like his mother and close friends vs. the one he painted in his rhymes, there exist stark contrasts. We cannot ignore these contrasts if we truly seek to know who Christopher Wallace was beneath all the hype and hip-hop gangsta glory. A brilliant rhyme smith? No doubt. One of hip-hop's greatest urban storytellers? Absolutely. But was Biggie rapping about what happened to him or what happened around him? The distinction is important, because perhaps if it really was more the latter, Christopher Wallace might be more credible in terms of being a true ghetto advocate, in a historical light.

His mother, Voletta Wallace, has insisted in almost every interview she's ever done, both during his life and following his tragic passing that her son was never denied a single material thing growing up, nor have his friends attempted to counter this. More importantly, Voletta Wallace has stated as firmly as a mother might to her child that Biggie was never allowed to leave the front stoop of his house, until well into his teens.

Perhaps then, the Notorious B.I.G. persona was just that, a personification of everything that went on around him in the urban Brooklyn neighborhood that he grew up in—of all its shady characters, the drug dealers, the pimps, the street thieves and the assassins. Perhaps, Biggie did witness many of the hard times he so vividly described in his lyrical tales on tape, *witnessed,* rather than participated in or experienced first hand.

This is also why parts of his rhymes, at times, seemed fantastical…as vivid as comic books or cinema. Still with so much left to the listener's imagination, Biggie's persona was that much more amplified. His rhymes were so descriptive and believable that one could literally close their eyes and envision Biggie in the circumstance, gun in hand, in a scene reminiscent of *Scarface* or the *King of New York*. One might argue that Biggie was living out his own ghetto fantasies in his raps, which in some instances, were so over-the-top that they literally became incredible.

Still, in order to succeed as a rap star, especially to represent as hard for Brooklyn as the city actually was, Biggie had to become a ghetto-superman, an all-powerful, all-encompassing set of eyes and ears that had heard and seen it all first hand. He had to become a hustler who had both lived and survived the tough upbringing of so many inner-city young black males.

In Biggie's rhymes, there were threads of the real man, the player— no one will deny Christopher Wallace his way with the ladies— interwoven with various pieces of characters and stories that would have been almost impossible for one single person to have lived in a single lifetime, especially at the tender age of 21, despite the fast pace of the inner-city. Perhaps Biggie is better then viewed as a representative because he was truly an advocate, and by speaking in a unified voice on behalf of millions of untold heroes of the everyday struggle, was therein that much more credible because we acknowledge this reality, and separate the man from the myth.

Wouldn't it better serve his legacy to read into his rhymes as a collection of stories told by many unsung voices through this one brave prophet, brave and bold enough to step up and represent as he did for the silent majority. For those who were too weak or worn down by their daily dealings with poverty, crime, societal racism, addiction, and all the other horrors that went on out of sight of larger society's blind eye.

Biggie had the gift of any inherently great prophet—to reach a mass number of people with his ghetto preaching. Christopher Wallace's words reflected the wisdom of a man who had seen it all, but perhaps in large part just that—seen—witnessed rather than personally experienced. He was freer to speak on what he had seen in this way, as he was following the urban code of naming no names; nor was he indicting himself in any prosecutable crimes.

Whether hip-hop listeners desire to admit it or not, many have wondered to themselves, how credible a rapper's claims of murder and assorted mayhem could actually be? In the case of 50 Cent, medical and criminal records confirm his credentials as an authentic player in the game. However, in the case of Biggie's arch nemesis, while he was living, rap legend Tupac Shakur...even his closest confidants have conceded that while Tupac grew up in abject poverty...much of his gangster persona was adopted following his riveting portrayal as Bishop in Juice. Tupac would go on to live what he rapped, racking up shoot-outs with the police, criminal convictions, and prison time prior to his untimely (or timely) demise as a victim of a drive-by shooting in 1996.

And as much as a comparison of the two is inevitable, given their friendship, rivalry, and the eerie similarities in their tragic murders—both in terms of the gangland style of the homicides and the fact that they both remained unsolved. The nature of their status as icons mirrors one another only in that they both were icons by the time of, and as a result of, their deaths.

The chief distinction within an analysis of their status as idols is the fact that most hip-hop historians agree that Tupac's death was a bit more anticipated and ultimately accepted than Biggie's. Tupac's fans were more desensitized to the prospect of his demise through volumes of raps in which he prepared his fans for his passing, prophesizing it, and proclaiming himself an *Outlaw Immortal*.

Tupac was an antagonist, even in his feud with Biggie, where Wallace played more of a defensive, diplomatic position. Tupac expected to die, whereas shortly before Biggie's death, in interviews and to friends, he was clearly thinking ahead toward his future—retiring in a short matter of years, watching his children grow up, becoming a label head himself. In other words, he had no idea what was coming around the corner. Nor did his fans, which made it that much more difficult to understand or make peace with.

What is even more frustrating in the years that have passed since the death of the Notorious B.I.G. than the lack of credible answers into who killed him and why, are those in the media and groupie-circles who have sought to make a name and a dollar off the inherent mystery surrounding Small's murder. Like circling vultures, they move round and round seeking to confuse us rather than provide us any answers, further littering an already disgusting (by-the-very-act) crime scene with their tabloid trash. Tupac had an extremely adversarial relationship with the media, and in the wake of his death, it's no wonder why.

An entire mini-industry has flourished out of the deaths of Tupac Shakur and the Notorious B.I.G., besieging all legitimate attempts to explore possible motives or true culprits behind both murders with a barrage of conjecture and regurgitated fantasy designed to make a fast buck and further confound an already confused nation of hip-hop fans.

A prominent example of the latter being the inflammatory tabloid-like documentary 'Biggie and Tupac', which achieved little more than lodging slanderous and largely circumstantial accusations at Death Row Records' C.E.O. Marion 'Suge' Knight, who the L.A.P.D. has exonerated as a suspect in masterminding the murder.

It is widely known that Knight employed off-duty L.A.P.D. officers to work security at Death Row events, and that several were also corrupt in their off time as well, namely Rafael Perez, David Mack, and the late Kevin Gaines, all of whom were part of the L.A.P.D. Rampart police corruption scandal. Still, director Nick Broomfield desperately attempts to link the coincidence of the officers' employment with Knight in their off time to the fact that they also did criminal activities while off-duty. Never mind the fact that he does so while never providing any substantive link between the Officers' employment with Knight and their criminal activities, than the fact that they both activities happened while the officers were out of uniform.

In reality, what Broomfield attempts is reckless, grossly irresponsible and inflammatory, and serves only to trample on both deceased rappers' graves by exploiting their memories to make a few dirty dollars. At no point, does Broomfield present any credible witnesses to back up his allegations, just convicted felons and disgruntled former police officers looking for 15 minutes of fame. Most notably, in the case of former Detective Russell Poole, who reigns as the king of conjecture and slander in this tabloid documentary.

What makes Poole and Broomfield's co-conspiracy so sickening is their manipulation of Biggie's mother, Voletta Wallace, who, rightfully desperate for answers to who murdered her beloved son, is unwittingly conned into participating in this witch-hunt. Aside from offering frustration at the lack of results from the elongated investigation into her son's slaying, providing some naturally fascinating atmospheric behind-the-scenes access into Biggie's condo, which she now occupies, as well as sharing some fond memories of her and Christopher's loving relationship, little else is accomplished with her involvement. None of the faces are new, nor are any of the answers Broomfield claims to provide.

What's worse, Broomfield spends the first hour plus of the documentary laying out the foundation for his accusations against Knight as mastermind to the murder of Biggie Smalls. And, in a more guarded way, Tupac, once he finally catches up with Knight at Mull Creek State Prison, cowers away from directly confronting him about any of the transgressions he has alleged prior thereto throughout his trash documentary.

Aside from taking veiled shots at Suge in the voice-over, completed after filming was done, Broomfield does nothing to directly address or connect his allegations to the man himself once presented with an opportunity. Perhaps it was the gravity of the charges in the face of the man finally catching up with Broomfield once sitting across from Knight, or possibly the weight of Knight's own presence, that caused the director to back down? Ultimately however, because of his cowardice in what he had built up to be a confrontation with Knight, in which the facts might be revealed, there is no climax, nor any real answers. And, in the end what is revealed is the flimsiness in Broomfield's entire argument-, which, is both laughable and ultimately self-defeating.

While most agree any study of the life of Biggie Smalls must address his death, the majority of the material that has come out since Wallace's passing in 1997, has focused almost exclusively on the latter. The only thing that has been conclusively proved regarding the murder of the Notorious B.I.G. is the fact that Suge Knight was most likely not involved. That Knight has refused to speak out on either Tupac or Biggie's murders, other than to call the allegations that he was the party responsible for either 'laughable', makes him an unlikely ally of his one-time nemesis, Sean 'P. Diddy' Combs, who has also refused to publicly speculate on who was responsible for the death of his best friend and marquee label act.

Even more ironic is the fact that both Combs and Knight were eyewitnesses to the deaths of Smalls and Shakur respectively. Neither will discuss the homicides beyond describing the last moments of both rappers' lives BECAUSE THEY LIKELY HAVE NOTHING MORE TO SAY! They know nothing more than what they have shared, and that they were each willing to volunteer the painful descriptions they did of Tupac and Biggie's last moments is commendable in and of itself.

Neither man will speak, out of respect for the dead; it's really that simple. There is nothing to hide, no mystery, other than the natural one both Knight and Combs are likely as confounded and confused by...as anyone else who bothers to ponder either man's murder or respective legacies...as they were affected by the rappers' deaths. No one ever bothers to wonder how painful it must have been for either Suge or Sean, as human beings, to watch their best friends die before their eyes and in their arms.

What American journalists like Broomfield and Randall Sullivan via *Rolling Stone Magazine* have preferred to do is, instead, suggest that, in Knight's case, he was responsible for arranging the murder of Shakur. How callous. In the case of the Notorious B.I.G., LA Times reporter Chuck Phillips even went as far as to suggest that Biggie paid to have Shakur killed, despite the fact that more than a half dozen witnesses place Wallace in New Jersey at the time, watching a prize fight, including best friend Lil Cease.

Mind you his article cited no sources on-record...all were conveniently anonymous. Ironic, too, that the First Amendment could not ultimately protect Biggie or Tupac from their own prophesies about dying at the hand of a player-hater, but that player-haters like Nick Broomfield and Chuck Phillips are protected by that very Amendment, as they make their slanderous and unfounded accusations.

Among Knight's only public comments on the allegations that he played a role in masterminding either Biggie or Tupac's murders, to date, has been a statement issued while he was still incarcerated in response to the Rolling Stone Magazine article which suggested his complicity in said murders. Knight's lawyer points out that "the Chief of the LAPD, Bernard Parks, was recently quoted as believing the Rampart case has been exploited by the media and police critics, and is being 'distorted beyond all proportion,' and also that according to Chief Parks, 'Officer Poole had some theories that could not be substantiated. He only brought it up when he left the department and after he had been personally disciplined and removed from the task force."

What justice are we doing Biggie to continually indulge tabloid journalists like Broomfield and Phillips? By physically spending money and buying their stories, we aren't literally doing so, but we might as well be, and that is the greatest injustice we could ever do either Shakur or Wallace. It's likely that the only way people like Broomfield sleep at night is to dream up more of this crap, and who can say who his next victim will be? It could be you.

Nevertheless, in the end, it is important to get any discussion of the death of Christopher Wallace out of the way in the beginning of this story. Then, we may do him the greatest justice we can—by celebrating his life and times, rather than focusing on the mystery surrounding his death, since it can lead nowhere new.

There is no mystery surrounding Biggie's celebrity; he was a natural star, born to become the icon he became and remains. He came from a loving home in spite of his harsh societal surroundings, and we carry him in our memory's heart and in our CD players because we too loved him as fans. His star naturally outshines the darkness surrounding his death, and ultimately, despite his natural contradictions as a human being, his long-term goal as a superstar was clear. He wanted to become, by the end of his career, the King of New York.

While Biggie, by his own admission in interviews, saw at least another 10 years in front of him in 1997 before he would get there—in the end, he did so in the span of 4. In "*The King of New York: The Biography of the Notorious B.I.G.*", we celebrate the life and times of a legend. This examination will be as honest as possible, pointing out both the strengths and flaws in Biggie's persona, in an attempt to understand the man behind the facade.

None of the interviews in this study will be anonymous, nor will there be any further theorizing about possible motives and/or responsible parties for Wallace's death. That is the job of the Los Angeles Police Department, not the news media. And, it will not be the responsibility of this author, for it would be an irresponsibility to attempt any further supposition into the who, where, what, why, or how? Dealing with what we know about the life of this remarkable icon, a much more revealing story will be told.

"I been in this game for years,
it made me a animal
There's rules to this shit,
I wrote me a manual
A step-by-step booklet for you to get
your game on track,
not your wig pushed back...
Number four: know you heard this before
Never get high, on your own supply
Number five: never sell no crack where you rest at
I don't care if they want a ounce, tell em bounce
Number six: that god damn credit, dead it
You think a crackhead payin you back, shit forget it
Seven: this rule is so underrated
Keep your family and business completely separated
Money and blood don't mix like two dicks and no bitch
Find yourself in serious shit,
Number ten: a strong word called consignment
Strictly for live men, not for freshmen
If you ain't got the clientele say hell no
Cause they gon want they money rain sleet, hail, snow..."

Ten Crack Commandments—Biggie Smalls

Chapter 2
Ten Crack Commandments

Being a former drug dealer in modern day is a required component of the generic hard-core rap artist's job description. That's because hip-hop, in its root, is urban expressionism, depicting abject poverty that, among other tragic by-products, led to the drug epidemic as a means of temporary escape, providing for some the additional hardship of drug addiction, and for others, ironically, a different sort of escapism—not (voyeuristic), but rather financial.

Where $3.75 an hour minimum wage didn't cut it anywhere in America, be it in the rural trailer park or the inner-city housing project, in the 1980s the crack epidemic took off in the former community at a time when a conservative presidential administration was looking for a media scapegoat to pin America's drug problem on...and the black community was the perfect patsy.

Never mind the fact that by 1987, at the height of the crack epidemic, America was spending $100 Billion dollars a year getting high, and only 25%, roughly, of that statistic was legitimately attributable to inner city crack sales. The other three-fourths of the drug buying population were largely white Americans between the ages of (21 and 28) celebrating the stock boom of the latter 1980s with cocaine abuse that was only unnoticed in the media because of its upper-middle class sales demographic.

Just as with the nightly news footage of the 'Black Welfare Mother', the media also burned the image of the 'Teenage, Black Crack Dealer' into the minds of suburban white America, making Regan Republicans feel safe in the illusion that the drug epidemic was not their problem. Back in the inner cities of America, however, where the financial effects of 'Trickle-Down Economics' had been only harsh and negative, for the young African American male, the occupation of crack dealer provided one of the only legitimate opportunities, albeit illegal, to make any real money.

While the media also loved to depict the average inner-city crack dealer as a decadent, free-spending wheeler-dealer who dressed like a pimp and drove an exotic sports car (Rolls Royce and the Corvette were Hollywood favorites), they regularly failed to document the domestic side of the crack dealer's life, which involved supporting out-of-work families, often in place of an absentee father, and often not only their own children, but also siblings and parents or grand parents.

One thing the media did get right was the violent side of the inner-city drug trade, largely trafficked among gangs that battled for territory with high-powered weaponry only otherwise seen in Rambo-esque Hollywood action films or historic war combat reels.

Hip-hop was the first forum to give the inner city drug dealer a personality. It was depicted as an average, everyday persona that addressed both the upsides (most commonly, women and the money to buy trendy clothes, jewelry) and the perils (death from gang violence, as a result of the drug trade; criminal charges and jail sentences that stemmed from the like; and addicted family members—girlfriends, and friends, among other topics). This described the psychology of the criminal persona that the young, black male had been branded with in the later 1980s by the American media.

In some ways, rap as an art form glorified the aforementioned persona, in others, it strove to portray it as an unavoidable norm—but one thing hip-hop performers rarely did, possibly in an effort to rebuke the media's popular trend, was judge it. Hence the birth of 'reality rap', an attempt on the part of hip-hop performers who were a product of the inner city to say to larger America, 'Here's the story behind the images, you've never heard it before, and we aren't seeking your judgment, or even your sympathy…only your understanding.'

In the early years of hip-hop, only generic attention was paid lyrically to the crack trade, but white America for the first time got a glimpse inside the world of the crack-dealer, and found it to be a largely dark, paranoid and unglamorous. This was contrary to the Nightly News stories of inflated street prices of Cocaine, which by the time they actually 'tricked down' to the lower-level inner-city dealers, were broken up into crack cocaine form, and sold in small quantity by corner peddlers. Peddling crack was, in fact harder work than the Miami Vice drug-dealer could ever imagine.

Most impoverished African American drug users never had the money to purchase the large quantities of Cocaine that were depicted on Friday night television; and the bigger dealers were usually required to maintain a heavy presence within their own impoverished communities to keep control over territory. As such, few ever had opportunity to buy the beach front houses seen on T.V., and at best were left with trendy inner-city fashions and expensive sports cars as trophies of their success.

East Coast rap artists like the Sugar Hill Gang and Grand Master Flash, in the early 1980s, had introduced music listeners to hip-hop first as a musical art form, and then as a social medium that extended itself beyond the topic of partying, and into the forays of inner city poverty. They were touching on the drug epidemic but not exploring it as a subculture. But, later-1980s rap artists from the West Coast, like Ice T and N.W.A. gave the landscape of the inner-city drug trade and the psychology of the drug dealer a more vivid and explicit exploration via landmark albums like '*Rhyme Pays*' in 1986 and '*N. W.A. and the Posse*' in 1987, and of course, the seminal '*Straight Outta Compton*' in 1988. After this, the world of 'Gangsta Rap' itself became a product, marketed directly to the now-very-curious audience of young suburban White America.

It was, ironically, one of the first times young black males had ever had a chance to connect as a peer group with young white males. And ironically, the medium of Gangsta rap, in an attempt to explain itself as a byproduct of a larger tragedy—that of inner-city poverty—became suddenly celebrated in ways that its fore-fathers, the crack dealers who created the reality proto-type that Gangsta rap followed, never naturally intended outside of their immediate neighborhoods.

With the over-night success of N.W.A.'s '*Straight Outta Compton*', which sold 2 million copies with no airplay in less than 6 months, featuring street hits like '*Fuck the Police*' and '*Dope Man*', the young black male was now presented with an alternative means to escaping the poverty of the ghetto, via the dream of making it legitimately as a rap star, and for the first time without having to hide where he had come from.

In a way it was therapy for a scapegoated generation, and aside from professional athletics, which up to that time had been one of the only alternative avenues to establishing a sense of self-worth outside of belonging to a gang, hip-hop now allowed a medium in which roots could be escaped without being forgotten. It gave a generation of beleaguered young, black males hope in the face of what amounted to a modern day conspiracy within the context of Reaganomics to fiscally oppress African America at large.

Hip-hop was the most potent form of protest African Americans had at their disposal since the Black Panther movement; and because of its commerciality, it was unstoppable in a way that no social movement had been prior thereto.

By the early 1990s, 'Gangsta Rap', largely via the soundscapes of hard core Godfather Dr. Dre and the West Coast powerhouse label Death Row Records, had become a multi-million dollar industry. Where Death Row Records dominated the gangland end of hardcore rap, the East Coast had brought culture and historical reference to the genre via seminal street intellects like KRS-One and Public Enemy, who treated hip-hop as a social cause for their people's struggle with poverty.

Additionally, however, underground founders like Southern rap lord Scarface, who took his name from the famed Al Pacino drug lord character, achieved gold record status chronicling the specifics of the crack trade as it had never before been attempted. Where N.W.A. and Ice T had helped to invent and perfect the generic Gangsta Rap formula, hip-hop artists like Scarface gave it the science of specifics, laying the groundwork for an entire subculture of hardcore rap focused almost exclusively, to the point almost of priding itself, on the inner-workings of not only selling crack, but also specifically how the business worked.

This extended itself to how a dealer went about acquiring its raw components—cooking it and breaking it down into smaller quantities to sell on the street corners of the inner city; how the mathematics worked within that formula—what was considered a successful transaction; what the authentic lingo within drug dealer culture was; what the daily schedule of a dealer might be like; how police were avoided; how addicts were dealt with, in the course of transactions; how the chain-of-command broke down within the ranks of larger-to-small time neighborhood drug dealers; and most significantly, how a drug dealer felt about his occupation in terms of its adverse effects on his own community in contrast to the positive ones within his own life.

All of the aforementioned contributed to a grander understanding of how the drug trade contributed specifically to inner city poverty and violence, as it never had before. No one had truly touched on it before artists like Scarface, at the turn of the year 1990; and as the decade began to unfold, mainstream hip-hop listeners began to pay more attention.

In a way, hip-hop as a sound, was itself a narcotic. Suburban white listeners started out hearing it in small doses—a single or album at a time, gaining access to bits at a time. They were brought into a fast-lane lifestyle, that Black kids near their own age lived day in and day out, and that they had only seen in movies like 'Boyz in the Hood' or 'Menace to Society'.

By the time the Notorious B.I.G. came along in 1994, the white kids had a craving for its specifics that could only be comparable to a drug users' need to try harder drugs. As they become more addicted, drug users would be moving from marijuana to L.S.D. to more intense highs brought on by Methamphetamines like Speed and Cocaine …and finally…Crack.

'Gangsta Rap' by 1994 had been popularly refined to the point where it was comparable in drug analogies to the Suburban white record buyer's Crack. They craved it, had to have it…in as large and vivid a dosage as possible…as much at a time as they could consume…without the slightest hint of exaggeration.

The latter demand within Gangsta rap's market made its purveyors work that much harder, producing in the process a new breed of superstar, an archetype who lived what he rapped, in real time if possible—hence early 1990s rap phenomenons like Snoop Dogg, who was charged with First Degree Murder the week his album debuted atop Billboard's Top 200 Album Chart, and Tupac Shakur, who was in jail following a sexual assault conviction (and a week-old ambush in which the rapper was shot five times) during the same week his third album, '*Me Against the World*' debuted atop the same album chart.

In that light, as it had become taken for granted by the early 1990s, that every Gangsta rapper originated from the ghetto, it also had become commonly assumed that every rap artist who rhymed about belonging to a gang or dealing drugs had actually done so. The latter was among Gangsta rappers' most popular claims toward the end of authenticity, and literally a requirement for mainstream acceptance among most suburban, white record buyers.

Still, critics had also begun to take notice, in some cases questioning the backgrounds of newcomers like Vanilla Ice, a white rapper who rapped in his rhymes about selling drugs, carrying a nine millimeter hand gun, and coming from an inner-city background, and claiming the same in interviews, when in fact investigative journalists later revealed he was a car washer who had grown up in a middle-class suburb in Texas.

African American rappers were more insulated, and got a greater benefit of a doubt from critics, but the bar was none-the-less raised to sharpen the accuracy and specifics of the day-ins and outs of any lyrical content touching on popular topics, like a ghetto-upbringing or former occupation within the drug trade.

To that end, when the Notorious B.I.G. first came on the scene, he revealed himself in both interview and song to be a former crack dealer, and offered evidence in support of that claim. He included the specific avenues and cross streets he sold on in Brooklyn, his specific clientele, and a large assortment of smaller supporting facts, notably including the fact that he had to hide the more expensive clothing that he bought with drug profits on the roof of his apartment building so his mother wouldn't find them and question him on the source of his money.

Some took Biggie's claims at face value. Still, on closer examination, there exist within Biggie's accounts, minor contradictions when compared to those of friends and family members of the rapper's lifestyle growing up. For example, in one of his raps, Biggie claims to "know how it feels being young from the slums, eating five-cent gums, not knowing where your meal's coming from".

Yet, as a close friend remembers, Biggie's mother doted on her only child growing up, spoiling young Christopher Wallace, such that "I bought him a radio. He wanted the best …Sharp or Sony. Anything Christopher asked for at Christmas, I made sure he had it," though he claimed in another rhyme that he "used to wonder why Christmas missed us, birthdays was the worst days."

Ultimately, in sorting the fact from fiction, in the reality behind Biggie's persona as a crack dealer, we can likely conclude that, at some point in his later teenage years, he did in fact begin selling crack. He most probably did it behind his mother's back, and as a result of peer pressure, rather than because of any material lacking within his own home life.

This is the most believable explanation in the face of the statistical reality that many young, black males from America's inner city neighborhoods fell party to this trade at some point in their later adolescence. Some would avoid it via athletics, others via good, old-fashioned schoolwork, but many fell into the trap. That most feel the Republicans had helped to set, because of the natural combination of peer and financial pressures that were prevalent in the inner city.

The important point to make in acknowledging this reality head-on was, that very little of it was actually the fault of the dealers, nor the addicts who they supplied. In fact, society at large was very much to blame, and only started to really listen when hip-hop became a commercial industry.

Biggie Smalls was indeed one of rap's foremost spokesmen, and he helped to give a face and a justification to the plight of the anonymous young black male hustling on America's corners day after day, putting his life on the line to feed a child or put a roof over his and often times his family's head.

White America had chosen for decades prior, to ignore this reality, living in the suburbs, oblivious to the hells African Americans faced day in and out, with the exception of sound bites on the evening news or on CNN. With the advent of hip-hop as a commercial property, those who had turned a deaf ear were now quickly coming to attention as their children were beginning to buy rap music and emulate hip-hop culture in the suburbs. There was no turning back, for rap's growing audience, nor for its newest sensation, the Notorious B.I.G.

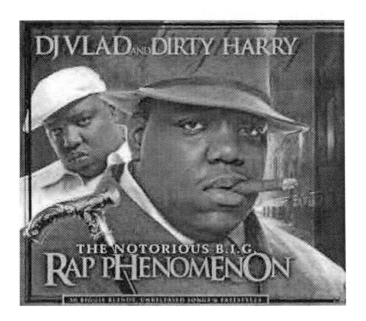

While he developed his skill and persona on the street corners, fate had a turn in mind for Biggie that was a far away destination from the dead end one he had grown up believing was his. And, as he approached his eighteenth birthday, he would begin his transformation from Christopher Wallace to the Notorious B.I.G.

—Jake Brown

Chapter 3
Christopher Wallace vs. Biggie Smalls

Just like rap's millions of young fans, Christopher Wallace, too, was at one time an impressionable teenager, soaking up the same inner-city culture his young fans later would, when he rapped about it on his debut album '*Ready to Die*'. Where fans saw it on videos and in lyrical imagery through Biggie's songs, young Christopher would undeniably see it all first with his own eyes.

Whether he lived part or all of it, or just was a very studious observer—likely a combination of both the latter and the former—he was still developing an alternate personality in his head, that would embody a little of everything he saw off the street from his stoop in the Bedford Stuyvesant section of Brooklyn, New York. As Biggie's mother Voletta Wallace explained, "My rule for him was he had to stay at the stoop...play right in front so I could see him. I trusted my son; it's just the street I never trusted."

As a result, Biggie Smalls as a persona, matured as Christopher Wallace grew into a perceptive teenager, who, by the admission of another close childhood friend Chico Del Vec, " Every day I'd see him at the same time in that same spot (on his stoop.) One day I was like 'Yo, come with me around the corner and meet some of my old timers, and he was like 'Alright.' And he was standing there, like, in shock."

Christopher Wallace undeniably grew up in an inner-city section of Brooklyn, but he never resided in a housing tenement, as he claimed in one rhyme, "celebrating every day no more public housing." Rather, he grew up in a comfortable two-bedroom apartment, though he was raised in a fatherless home by a single mother who worked two jobs to provide for herself and her only son.

Additionally, as Biggie's mother remembered, Biggie as a child used to vacation to his mother's native Jamaica, wherein "we would go to Jamaica every year. Christopher loved the Reggae beat. He had an uncle who was a DJ, and on Saturdays Christopher would go to clubs (with his uncle) and play the music."

In many ways, Biggie Smalls was more scrutinized in points like the latter because he was considered the first all-encompassing Gangsta rap superstar. His subject matter could range from the drug deal to the dance floor, and within the same sound scope, from the pressure of being a young father to the pleasure of being a player. Toward that end, Biggie had a lot of ears to please with his debut, and on tape, perhaps rapped with a broader brush than he might have intended people paint him with as an individual, off tape and in the course of his every-day life.

He admitted as much to one journalist, explaining that "nobody that buys *Ready to Die* knows me, they just know the Notorious B.I.G.; and that's all I really want them to know. Everybody needs their privacy, everybody needs their own time to be to themselves." Still, in another breath, Biggie told a journalist profiling the rapper very early on in his career that "my shit comes off so strong and my hardness is so sincere because I've lived all that shit."

In reality, it was because Biggie Smalls gave so much of himself to his first album's subject matter that he opened himself to a certain amount of scrutiny. What he claimed were the specific struggles of his daily life, more importantly, were analogous to those of his larger community. There is no doubt, that as he grew older, Biggie, no matter how impoverished or not, had grown up as Christopher Wallace the child. And, he became immersed to a verifiable degree in the street hustle that surrounded him within his Bedford Stuyvesant neighborhood.

It is here, beginning in Wallace's later teens, that any credible study of Biggie's exposure to the street life and specifically, the crack trade, prior to becoming a rap star should begin. While Biggie claimed on record and in many interviews that he hustled because he had no other genuine opportunity to get ahead financially, he was clearly immersed in the lifestyle for reasons that weren't entirely professional. "Hustlers were my heroes. Everything happened on the strip I grew up in. It didn't matter where you went, it was all in your face."

Biggie's personal interest, as a child, in the lifestyle of the hustler was understandable, given his exposure to it at such an impressionable age. While he would play it out later, as a character on record and in front of the cameras, in what was a more mainstream personification of the hustler image that mixed a potent combination of fantasy and reality, the generation of viewers who would idolize him were as young and equally as impressionable as he had first been when he began sculpting the alter-ego that would later become The Notorious B.I.G. Therein, while it was sometimes hard to decipher the fact from fiction in the background Biggie painted for journalists, in the course of selling his dominant hustler persona, it would ultimately matter less and less as his stardom dawned, and the line between fantasy and reality became more and more blurred in the glare of Biggie's rising star.

Looking back on the block in later years, however, Biggie would do his best to paint the impression that he was a "full time 100 percent hustler. (I was) sellin' drugs...My mother goin' to work would see me out there in the morning. That's how I was on it."

Biggie's mother didn't totally dispute his claims, only attempting to qualify the degree to which he was realistically involved in the hustler lifestyle. "He was only a small-time dealer, making a few dollars here and there…He was arrested for carrying a gun without a license and he spent three days in jail when he ignored the summons to appear in court."

It was in fact Biggie's friend Damien 'D Roc' Butler, who took the credit for Biggie's weapon possession, earning 3 years in prison in what he recalled as a matter of sacrifice for the sake and health of Biggie's career, "We was walking, and he was like 'Man, all I need to do is go 'Gold'. I can't believe I got a deal.' And the police had rolled up on us, and they (found a gun Big had ditched), and took us both down to the precinct. And the cop was like 'Yo, there's two of you, and I'm not taking two people down for one gun. I'ma give y'all a minute to figure it out.' And I was like 'Yo, you got a record deal, I don't got a record deal. I'll take the weight, you just do your thing' (And I ended up serving 3 years)."

As a rap star, Biggie's stories of struggle would fluctuate from interview to interview, offering the same general tale, wherein the rapper spent his days "on the corner, selling drugs with my niggas." It was still with inconsistencies that wouldn't have gone noticed at the time, but upon closer inspection, revealed a more realistic variation of the truth wherein Biggie was indeed a drug dealer. But, perhaps Biggie dealt more casually than the hardest core of rap fans or critics would have found to be up to par with the larger-than-life persona his role as The Notorious B.I.G. required him to portray.

In this regard, while Biggie would claim in one generic breath that he was "waking up early in the morning, hitting the set selling my shit at the crack of dawn. My mother goin' to work would see me out there in the morning," he would also give more specific recountings of his actual daily routine that reflected that of the average young black male's, rather than that of the mythic super-gangster rapper he was saddled with playing in the press.

From the latter angle, a more realistic view of Biggie's daily routine as a hustler was "basically…the same thing (day after day), waking up around nine o'clock so you can catch the check-cashing place at nine-fifteen, nine-thirty. I didn't have checks, but the crackheads did." Most listeners, regardless of their level of affiliation with the drug trade, responded to Biggie's raps in kind, concluding that B.I.G. did in fact have enough basic knowledge of the ins and outs of the 'hustler' lifestyle and mentality to qualify him as, at the very least, acceptable, and in most cases, celebrated spokesman on their behalf.

For his own part, in most cases, Biggie stuck to the typical hustler's had-no-choice-in-the-matter rationale, arguing that, in the course of hustling, "I did what I had to do. Hustle, rob, whatever. I always wanted to be a fly nigga, always wanted to have a lot of money. I knew sitting on my ass wasn't going to make it. Mom duke wasn't going to give it to me. School, yeah, maybe some shit would have progressed, who knows?"

According to Biggie's mother, however, Christopher Wallace, into his early teenage years, attended (a private, Catholic school), made close to straight A's, and was a well-mannered young man who came from a good home, "(From age 6 on), Christopher went to St. Peters Claver. He had the English Award, the Math Award, the Reading Award, every award you can think of." Still, even Voletta Wallace had to eventually step toe-to-toe with the peer pressure Biggie was feeling out on the block, such that, as she recalled, she eventually threw her hands up when Biggie made the decision to drop out in 11th grade.

Instead she took a defensive pose with her son, based on the statistical probabilities he faced as a young, black male out on the street corner, now that those realities would face him directly as a high-school drop out. Christopher's mom recalled that he had told her, "Mom, you went to school, you went to college, but that's not me right now." He saw something out there (on the street) that fascinated him…It was that fear of the street (for me). I didn't know what was going on out there. So the first thing I did was put life insurance out on my son."

Whether Biggie then got into hustling because he had to, or out of peer pressure, or, perhaps as a result of both, he still became immersed in the lifestyle for better or worse as he progressed into his teenage years, venturing off the stoop of his apartment building to find "real niggas. You know (where) there ain't no tall tales. I think every corner goes through the same drama our corner goes through. It was just niggas hustling—regular kids with a philosophy of 'Let's just get the money.'"

Biggie identified his primary corner for operation as Fulton Street and Washington (Avenue), in Brooklyn, and whatever he may have occasionally downplayed in terms of the extremity of his own involvement in selling crack, he provided no shortage of stories concerning other exposures he had experienced to the violence inherent in the inner-city environment he grew up in, claiming to one journalist that he had first seen someone shot at the tender age of "fifteen or sixteen. I really didn't get to see no blood squirtin'. All I know is we was runnin' and we was chasin' this nigga. The nigga says, 'Stop!' and I heard a shot: Pow! I saw a dude drop. My man put the gat to his head, somebody screamed 'Run!' and we all ran. This was just real. It was nothin'. We were seeing niggas gettin' hit all the time."

In another instance, Biggie claimed to a journalist that he had watched a man die in his arms, recalling that "my man Cheese, God bless him. He died in my arms in the subway station at Clinton and Washington…(I didn't see him get shot.) He was downstairs in the station and we were upstairs on the corner hustling. We just heard two loud shots. Sounded like cannons: Boom! Boom! We ran downstairs and saw Cheese just spread out. I felt fucked up. I thought, My man is gonna die. No one wants a nigga to die."

Biggie preferred to keep the stories of his street background larger than life, much like his persona required he do on record, "Oh, we're in the land of the lost, man. We drop you in our part of town with a blindfold, man, you won't be doing all the other stuff that people be doing. People look at Brooklyn as motherfuckin' thievery and larceny, trite shit, you know? But we don't get down like that. At least my peoples. I mean, we may've had to do what we had to do, but it wasn't no shit we took as a profession, that we would keep doing. If we ever robbed somebody, it was to get enough money to get some work so we could flip it."

Still, while Biggie may have claimed not to have been directly involved in any of the often senseless violence that accompanies life in the inner city, he still appeared to have become desensitized to it during his teenage years, such that, by the time he had signed his record deal, at age 21, he revealed to one journalist that when on the block, "I'm expecting something to happen, because it's nothing special to me. It happens on every corner I go to in Brooklyn. I'm immune to it. The only time that hearing someone got killed is a surprise to me is when it's somebody I was close to. So then I have a feeling: I have mourning for them."

Despite Biggie's hardened exterior in interviews, most friends and family remember him as one of the funniest characters on the block. Through this lens, another side of Christopher Wallace emerges which is considerably lighter than the dark, ominous character he portrayed in the press; one in which we see glimpses of the versatility in Biggie as a person, wherein his appeal as a rapper came from his ability to both recount without remorse, as well as celebrate, the realities of the hustler lifestyle.

More importantly, Biggie's descriptions of the upsides to being a hustler allowed listeners to see that there was in fact a choice in the criminal lifestyle he led, mainly evident in the fact that he was cognizant of the wrong in what he was doing, and yet did it anyway, and not solely because he was forced to, but, to a degree, because he enjoyed it as well. "Even though it was dead wrong what I was doing, we still had mad fun."

While the latter admission erases some of the inherent sympathy for the plight of the young, black male, at least Biggie's representation of it, it still is important toward gleaning some insight into the other side of Wallace's life. It was this side of the rapper's day, when he wasn't out on the corner hustling solely to raise money to feed his young children, as he claimed in rhymes and in many interviews, but instead was taking that same money and "going shopping all the time…We was young, so we was just goin' to get jewelry and clothes and stay the flyest.

And the girls—there was the whole competition about the girls and who had the prettiest girlfriend. Then there was goin' to school, flyin' it with other fly niggas in school, and niggas gettin' motorcycles and niggas gettin' Honda Accords and [Jeep] Cherokees. We'd go to the movies on the weekends, go to 42nd Street with the fellas, bump into a whole bunch of girls, party…It was just on, you know what I'm sayin'? It was fun!"

In elaborating on his fonder memories of life growing up on the block, Biggie remembers "just being in the neighborhood and getting money and knowing that in other neighborhoods there's niggas getting money. It's like a little competition." Childhood friend Hubert Sam confirmed the latter, recalling that "Fulton St. was definitely free enterprise. Competition was at your front and back."

Lifelong friend and fellow hustler Chico Del Vec recalled Biggie's transition into the life of a street hustler as it authentically evolved, in the process aiding the evolution of Christopher Wallace's rap persona, Biggie Smalls, "We'd play dice, get money, get something to eat, ask anybody if they want to eat (and Big was always eating)…He didn't care, he'd see a girl…and go 'Give me a dollar, give me five dollars, buy me something to eat.'..(And) he was so big that everyone be afraid of him when he was the sweetest one in the crew."

As fellow hustler/crew member D Roc elaborated, "most of the older guys, they was callin' him Biggie Smalls because he was kind of chubby (and always eating)."

As Biggie matured as a street hustler in his later teenage years, he also met his first long-term girlfriend Jen Jackson, who eventually became pregnant with Biggie's first child, Tyanna. As she recalled the changing affect her birth had on Big, "before, it was all about him, him, him. (After the birth of Tyanna), he was all about 'My daughter, my daughter, my daughter.'" Friend and former manager Mister Cee remembered, Biggie adored his daughter, and sought to spoil her just as his own mother had when he was a younger child, "Its all he talked about—Tyanna, Tyanna, Tyanna, Tyanna. I wanna put carats in her ear, I want to get her a fur coat.

He loved that little girl. The birth of his daughter opened his eyes to drive him to be the best artist he could be." The birth made Wallace take everything more seriously in his life, despite his dreams to make it as a rap star, in the process pushing him toward risking it all out of what arguably for the first time in his life was hustling out of necessity to support his child. As his baby girl's mother, Jan Jackson, reasoned, "(B.I.G.'s) not going to sit around and wait for (someone) to say 'Here's $1000, go buy your daughter a crib.' I'm sorry, he's gonna go on the corner, and get that $900, and buy his daughter a crib."

By the time of his daughter's birth, Biggie had stopped disputing that selling drugs was a conscious choice on his part, rather a choice made in the face of desperation from little other financial means, by which to meet his obligations, including the birth of a baby daughter. As Biggie explained, by that time, he knew the implied risks to selling crack cocaine, and accepted the implied potential for consequences, including both the prospect of death and jail time, in the face of what could prove to be the only avenue toward reaping any real financial successes coming out of the projects of Brooklyn.

"A man always has a choice. I was fucked up in the game for a nice little piece. I wasn't stressed, but I wasn't where I wanted to be. Any young nigga growin' up in the 'hood don't want just average 9 to 5 paper. I mean how far is that going to last? How's 9 to 5 paper gonna pay for a Lexus? How's it gonna pay for Versace, Moschino and Armani and all that shit? That's what you want if you want to be a baller! You wanna ball with the rest of them niggaz! I knew the 9 to 5 wasn't gonna do it. The drug game was doing it to a certain extent, but you know how the game go. Any nigga that's in it knows you gonna take your little falls here and there. That's part of the game. Any nigga that fall or slip and get upset about it is a fool 'cause you suppose to expect that type of bullshit!"

That Biggie can tie his reasoning for selling narcotics directly to a need to support his daughter makes his overall claim and credibility about living the hustler life that much more valid in the face of his mother's loving upbringing, in which Christopher Wallace had been thoroughly provided for materially. It is reasonable to believe that by a certain point, later into Biggie's teens, that he broke out from under his mother's protective watch, ventured off his front stoop, and began to soak up the game first-hand.

From this vantage point, it could then be concluded that a combination of experiences, some collected through observation as a bystander and others through actual personal ordeals, molded Christopher Wallace the person, and in turn, Biggie Smalls the rapper.

Still, despite the dramatic transition his life would take during this coming time, Biggie tried hard never to stray too far from the streets that would make him a star, telling one journalist later on that "I didn't really leave the streets behind. I try to chill with my niggas as much as possible." Regardless, Biggie's time had begun to come, and as he made his way from Brooklyn into Manhattan, from the street corner battles to the billboard charts and concert stages, he wouldn't forget where he had come from —the rule most hustlers regard as most consequential to making it out of the ghetto.

The latter vantage point preaches that because the streets made you who you are, good or bad, you have to acknowledge them as part of you—rapper, superstar athlete, or hustler. Biggie would not only acknowledge the borough he had come from, he would celebrate it in his music and image as the *King of New York* while he worked to put his beloved city back on the national hip-hop map.

"Nigga I'm the hardest nigga in hip-hop."

—Christopher Wallace, a.k.a. Biggie Smalls,
a.k.a. Notorious B.I.G.

Chapter 4

Exodus: From Christopher Wallace to Biggie Smalls to Notorious B.I.G.

The genesis of Biggie Smalls, from street hustler to hip-hop phenomenon, from Christopher Wallace to the Notorious B.I.G., began much in the vein of any rags to riches story. Only rather than overnight, it happened over many nights of crack slanging, gun toting, paranoia, and desperate decadence where, by the time he was discovered as a fledgling MC with the potential to become a superstar, Christopher Wallace already had established his reputation as a player, a father, and a convict.

One journalist reviewed the rapper's street credibility in a *Source* feature on the rapper, shortly following the release of his debut album, *Ready to Die*. "For years, he's stood as the Mayor-elect for St. James, holding down an area infamous for drugs and guns."

His charisma was as compelling, his style of rhyming as intoxicating as that of any rapper that Sean Puffy Combs had ever encountered as Vice President of A&R Uptown Entertainment up until that point. This was largely because East Coast hip-hop in the 1990s had lost its edge, and had not yet witnessed the rise of the decade's first true superstar. Within his potential, Sean Combs also faced a tremendous challenge in authenticating Biggie's life experiences into something palatable for the record buying masses. Such as it was, it took almost two years from the time that Combs signed Smalls 'til the formal release in mid 1994 of Notorious B.I.G.'s debut album, *Ready to Die.*

Ironically, Biggie Smalls never intended rhyming as his principle means of making a living. It started off as something of a hobby. One of Biggie's earliest experiments into publicly introducing himself as an MC in the neighborhood occurred at the basement house parties of his friend Mabusha 'Push' Cooper, who recalled that "we called (our party) Soul Powers 197, and people called it a basement party. And we would have an open mic session, and that's when Big started doing his thing…We were shocked, because here was this quiet, big guy that everyone always saw standing on Fulton St.—*rhyming*, and holding the flow…Big was notorious on the mic."

As Biggie himself described his early days as a fledgling MC, "I was always writing rhymes, but I wasn't trying to get me a record deal. niggaz used to tell me I was nice and everything, but these are the niggaz I'm always with every day, you know? I really couldn't take it as nothing…I put one hundred percent of my time into hustlin'… but at the same time, when I was waiting on corners, I'd hang out with niggaz and we'd go downstairs to the basement. This DJ, 50 Gran, he'd flip the records and just rock the instrumentals…I came in and said 'Yo, I get busy', and he was like, 'Yeah, right.' I picked up the mike and rhymed, and they were like 'Damn, he's nice.'…I'd just flow over the beats, and he started taping everything."

As DJ Mister Cee recalled the quality of the demo, "the tape that he brought me was just a home-basement demo, but I was blown away. Most of the time when I'd got demos, the rappers usually were not very good, but B.I.G. sounded like he'd been rhyming forever. One of the tracks even used the 'Blind Alley' sample that had been heard on (Big Daddy Kane's) '*Ain't No Half Steppin*'', and I had the same reaction listening to him that I had when I first heard Kane. It was just raw talent."

Even as others were beginning to see him as a potential superstar, Biggie, at the time, downplayed the demo as anything more than a glorified block battle, another chance to show people he had the skills, just no ability to see beyond his neighborhood in terms of where he could take his talent, "the demo was basically freestyle lyrics. Fifty…sixty bars of just straight rhyming over '*Blind Alley*,' EPMD instrumentals and shit like that. Just showing niggaz I had skills."

Taking on the early role as Biggie's manager, Cee arranged for a press kit, and signed the rapper to a production deal, allowing the two to begin collaborating on a more professional demo tape. It would eventually launch Biggie to stardom when it landed in the hands of Sean 'Puffy' Combs, who at the time was still working as Vice President of A&R at Uptown Entertainment.

As Cee recalled the early preparation of Biggie's demo and earliest publicity portfolio, they attempted to keep Biggie as close to the street as possible, "I knew we would need pictures for the (demo) package…I hired this dude, George DuBois, who had shot a few Big Daddy Kane album covers. Biggie took those pictures right on Bedford and Quincy avenues. That was the same spot where he hung out and smoked weed, so it was perfect."

While Cee fondly remembered Wallace's lighter side, he also recognized Biggie's potent combination of natural talent as a lyricist and authenticity as a hustler that would work to begin his ascent to the position as New York's hottest underground MC, "We had a lot of laughs that day…(On his demo,) he painted beautiful pictures with the simplest lyrics…He would put you inside the mind of the thug next door and explain why he sold drugs or why he was so stressed out…And once he started getting more confidence, it was over. "

Biggie's demo had first ended up in Combs' hands much by accident, via a friend of the rapper who had hustled on the same block, and spent free time battle-rapping with Wallace in the basement of an apartment building in Bed Stuy. As Biggie recalled, "(My boy Kane's) DJ, Mister Cee, heard one of (my) tapes, and told me about this shit in The *Source* called Unsigned Hype. I said 'Fuck It, send it in.' And (former Source Editor) Matty C loved it. He played it for Puffy."

According to *NME.com*, the series of events that led to the demo's circulation began in January, 1990, when "using the pseudonym 'Quest', then the 'Biggie Smalls' nickname, (Wallace) rapped with the Old Gold Brothers Crew and borrowed a couple of turntables, a mic, a mixer and a cassette deck to do some scratching and looping, and recorded himself over the breakbeats. (Over the course of 1990, developing his rap persona while still hustling, Biggie refines his skill as a fledgling recording artist, such that, by January, 1991), as Biggie Smalls, he does a freestyle for the Stretch Armstrong/Bobbito Show, broadcast on Columbia University radio station WKCR.

Word began to get around and a tape landed in the hands of Big Daddy Kane's Mister Cee, who passed the demo on to Dream Hampton, who at the time was editing *The Source*, America's #1 hip-hop magazine. The journalist liked the rough-and-ready rap style of Biggie and featured him in the magazine's Unsigned Hype column. Shortly thereafter, he recommended Wallace to Sean 'Puffy' Combs (aka Puff Daddy), who was Vice President of A&R at Uptown Records."

As Calvan "Mister Cee" Laburn recalled, "the first time I took Big to Puffy...I knew Big would be in good hands, because music wasn't just another job for Puffy; he lived it. His love for hip-hop (like Big) is evident." Still, at the time, Cee remembered, Biggie had no knowledge of Puffy's rising star as a producer, "at the time Puffy was still doing A&R at Uptown Records...Biggie didn't even know who he was, so I explained that Puff was the cat, who had worked with Mary J. Blige and Jodeci.

In the meeting, Puff asked Big to kick a rhyme. He sat there, excited, and when Big finished, Puff said, 'We can have a record out by the summer.' That's how fast it happened." As P. Diddy remembered his first encounter with Biggie, "I took him up to Sylvia's in Harlem, and he didn't eat. He wouldn't talk, he was real quiet. (And so I asked him to bust a rhyme right there on the spot, and when he started) I just didn't want him to stop. He sounded so good...so refreshing...it was like he was rapping, but it was so catchy. It was almost like he was singing. And he was such a clever poet, the way he put words together, the say he saw things."

Outside of opening up as a lyricist, Combs also recalled that Biggie was extremely shy...very much in his superstar infancy. "When I first met Biggie, he was real quiet and shy...He would barely talk, you know...like, I'd have to force him to talk to have a conversation with me. He would just be there observing. It was just that he didn't know that it was such a big deal to him. This was a dream come true to finally have a chance to be a rapper that, you know, I think he was overwhelmed by it. And, he just wanted to be quiet, and just you know, enjoy it. It's almost like if you talk too loud in a room somebody may kick you out. You know what I'm saying. I think he wanted to make sure he stayed in the room." This was likely due, at least in part, to the fact that Smalls' head was not in the clouds, rather his feet still planted very firmly in the street, and his immediate reality still very much that of a hustler.

In that light, while Biggie may have had the natural talent to become what he eventually did within the industry, and could show off that talent on cue, he still knew he was a million records and miles from the top. On a whole other, more commercially focused level, while Puffy remarked upon first hearing Biggie's rapping style, "It sounds like you could rhyme forever—I want to sign you." The reality was that most of the record buying public was not mentally preconditioned to accept the type of reality that Biggie espoused on his debut. More importantly, most emcees who had come out of the East Coast had never spoken as vividly as Biggie did about life in the ghetto in the present term, instead favoring war stories about things they may have allegedly grown up doing.

Notorious BIG was the real thing. He lived out his life as a gangster in real time, so authentically that, just a few days prior to his signing with Sean Combs, Biggie was living down south in North Carolina with his old crew, selling crack again. It had only been after an impassioned plea from Combs that B.I.G. had agreed to come back to New York in favor of signing onto Comb's label, over returning to the drug trade.

As P. Diddy remembered, "when I heard North Carolina, I knew what he was doing. So I tracked him down, and just begged him. I pleaded with him, 'Don't do this with your life. That's short money right there. Its not worth it.' And he told me (afterward), 'This better work out, I could have made a lot of money down there.'" The bottom line had been the money. Biggie had returned home from North Carolina on Puffy's assurances that his record deal was as solid as the day he had signed it.

Perhaps prophetically, the day after BIG came back to New York, the apartment Biggie had been staying in was raided by the local police narcotics unit. Only in retrospect has Biggie seemed to question whether staying would have been a bad move, even had he been picked up as part of the police sweep. He had faced jail time prior thereto—a nine-month stint in a local North Carolina jail on narcotics-related charges. Such that, by the second time such a prospect was nearing him, he escaped it based on a combination of luck, trademark smooth talking on Combs' part, and maybe, a little twist of fate.

As Biggie recalled the incident several years later to a journalist, "Puffy called me on a Monday, and told me that the contracts would be ready on Tuesday. He said 'Come on up, and I'll have the check waiting for you.' I was gonna stay till Tuesday because it was near the first of the month and we were gonna get those crack-head's welfare checks...The same night I was on the train coming back to New York, the cops ran up in our spot...It turns out the nigga that we didn't know had been on the run for over seven years, and the other two niggas that was with him got conspiracy charges."

What made Biggie more stressed out about his real prospects of making a living as a hip-hop star was his responsibility as a family man to support his daughter. He had financial realities that Combs' did not, although Puffy would soon, too, get a reality check of his own when he was fired from Uptown Entertainment, directly threatening B.I.G.'s deal, as well as his larger shot at making hip-hop history.

As Puffy recalled, "I went home and thought about killing myself. Then I went into my bedroom and went to sleep for like 10 hours. And when I woke up, I came out and checked my answering machine and there were messages from all the major labels offering me my own deal." While Biggie had already completed roughly half of what would be his debut album at the time of Combs' firing, the label was not sure if they wanted to keep Smalls on or not, as an artist without Combs' as his A&R man.

Combs, seeing the opportunity, negotiated to take Biggie with him to his new imprint, Bad Boy Entertainment, at Arista Records, under a $10 million joint-venture with Clive Davis. The year was 1992, and while the rest would be hip-hop history, Biggie Smalls would first have to endure a series of personal and professional hardships before he ever experienced his first real taste of what his eventual stardom would become.

His first exposure as an artist to the world of commercial hip-hop began with the brief rap he contributed in June, 1992 to a Puffy-produced remix of Mary J Blige's 'Real Love', which was a huge success at urban radio. Thereafter, Puffy featured him on (list remixes, etc) culminating with the early B.I.G. signature *'Party'* and *'Bullshit'*, whose inclusion on the soundtrack for the motion picture *'Who's The Man?'* led to its release as a club single, and subsequently made it one of early 1993's biggest hits.

At the same time Biggie was beginning his rise as an artist, Puffy was about to experience his temporary decline as a hip-hop mogul. The original contract Biggie signed with Sean 'Puffy' Combs was as an artist on Andre Harrell's MCA-distributed Uptown Entertainment. It was, at the time, one of the premier hip-hop forces on the East Coast during the West Coast rap renaissance led by Dr. Dre and Suge Knight's Death Row Records.

I got techniques drippin out my buttcheeks
Sleep on my stomach so I don't fuck up my sheets, huh
My shit is deep, deeper than my grave G
I'm ready to die and nobody can save me
Fuck the world, fuck my moms and my girl
My life is played out like a Jheri curl,
I'm ready to die!

—Biggie Smalls—*Ready to Die*

Chapter 5
Ready to Die

Christopher Wallace began to record what would become his groundbreaking debut, 'Ready to Die' in 1993. His on-record recounting of an inner-city upbringing was one resembling an unfortunate and disturbingly large number of African American children in today's America—fatherless homes in economically impoverished areas of inner cities all over the United States, so divided, and with living conditions so tragically predictable.

While Biggie's future as a hip-hop superstar was the last thing anyone could have predicted, his entry into the role of narcotics purveyor was as obvious as his motivations for doing so. Because his mother was a school teacher, Biggie's home life was relatively strict, such that, even in the face of the money he made as a hustler, he couldn't enjoy its fruits unless he was out on the block, and that much more vulnerable to competitors and haters alike. Still, Biggie, from an early age, wouldn't accept the limitations of the economic poverty he had been born into, instead seeking to defy them with material wealth, even if it meant defying his mother.

In his early days as a crack dealer, however, Biggie had to be as careful at home as he did on the corner, principally because according to Smalls he was still living under her roof. As he recalled to one journalist, "I couldn't bring any of my clothes to the house, 'cause my moms would flip…I used to hide all my shit on the roof of our building, leave for school in the busted shit my moms gave me, and change my whole outfit on the roof."

Once on the block, Biggie had spent his days as a high school drop out, hanging out with his crew of fellow hustlers, selling crack, mackin on women, and developing his style as an emcee. Biggie took in the urban realities of what he saw occurring around him on a daily basis as a hustler, processed those observations mentally and emotionally into a visual, verbal imagery, and spit them back out in a commercially-lethal format that could be taken in as naturally as oxygen by anyone listening.

Biggie spoke on a universal level, still with an honesty that didn't have to be qualified with a movie role or an interview loaded with testimonials from supposed criminal associates. Biggie spoke for himself, and for a generation of young, starving African American males who stood inevitably behind him, because, as he reasoned, "I guess…my music is so heartfelt…(because) that's not just me…There's a lot of niggas that going through the same situation like me, you know what I'm saying?"

By the time Biggie had graduated to the status of signed rap artist, the principle difference between he and most of those like him in the rap game was that, in recalling his upbringing as a crack dealer, he made no excuses for why he did it. He didn't blame it on societal ills more than he had to. He didn't blame it on anyone but himself in terms of his own ambition for something better, no matter the means. And strangely, he had an internal desire to keep close to the fire, live on the edge, push the arrow as far into the red as possible before running out of gas, or chances.

In comparing himself in the latter respect to fellow MCs, Biggie distinguished himself as that much more real by pointing out that the drama in his life as a rapper was very much his own doing, that he walked the same talk as an emcee that he had as a hustler, and that nothing had changed from his days as a hustler on the corners in Brooklyn in terms of his realness. "(Another rapper will be) into his family and his music—that's all he does.

Maybe if I chose to live that lifestyle, I wouldn't be involved in a lot of things. But my mother told me if there wasn't no drama, I wouldn't want to be a part of it. There got to be a little spice in it for me. That's my problem." Dating that tendency back to his teenage years, Biggie had dropped out of high school, and moved out of his mother's home, by age 17, devoting himself full time to the narcotics trade, both because he had to, and because he wanted to.

In establishing that fact on record, Biggie tended to lean toward the latter, suggesting that he had had no choice but to pursue the path of a hustler, but where he really resonated with listeners was in his descriptions of exactly why he was helpless but to be stressed. Wallace put a human face on the hustler that had not been illustrated to rap listeners prior thereto, and he did it in such a skillful manner that it became impossible to ignore, let alone argue with. "Shit, it's hard being young from the slums, eatin five cent gums not knowin where your meals comin from, Damn, what happened to the summertime cookouts? Every time I turn around a nigga gettin took out, Shit, my momma got cancer in her breast, Don't ask me why I'm motherfuckin stressed, things done changed."

Whether Biggie had personally lived every line he boasted on his album, he had certainly witnessed enough of the struggle in the community around him to be an authentic advocate for his people. His lyrics were completely desensitized to the existence of the harsh realities of the ghetto. They were accepted, yet he was aware of their consequences in almost every verse he rapped, "Dealin with the dope fiend binges, seein syringes in the veins… Hard to explain how I maintain…The crack smoke make my brain feel so strange…People look at you like you'se the user, Selling drugs to all the losers…But they don't know about your stress-filled day…Baby on the way mad bills to pay."

Still, to Wallace's credit, he was also able to admit his role and complicity in context of his desire to begin hustling, alternately to being motivated solely out of financial necessity, "I'm (in my teens), smokin' blunts, makin' cream, On the drug scene, fuck a football team, Riskin' ruptured spleens by the age of sixteen, Hearin' the coach scream at my lifetime dream, I mean I wanna blow up, stack my dough up, So school I didn't show up, it fucked my flow up, Mom said that I should grow up and check myself before I wreck myself, disrespect myself, Put the drugs on the shelf? Nah, couldn't see it—Scarface, King of New York, I wanted ta be it."

Another astonishing facet of Biggie as an MC was how multidimensional he was in his personality as a rapper, where he could go from the unapologetically violent "I wouldn't give fuck if you're pregnant. Give me the baby rings and a #1 MOM pendant" to the other extreme as a father "Livin' life without fear, Puttin' 5 karats in my baby girl's ears."

On another level entirely, Biggie picked up where LL Cool J had left off with 'I Need Love', recording what would eventually become his first number one record with '*One More Chance*', in which he depicted himself as rap's consummate player when it came to the ladies, both on wax and in the bedroom, such that "I get swift with the lyrical gift. Hit you with the dick, make your kidneys shift...I got the cleanest meanest penis, ya never seen this stroke of genius...Fuck whatcha heard who's the best in New York, fulfillin fantasies without that nigga Mr. Rourke? Sex gettin rougher when it come to the nut buster, Pussy crusher, black nasty motherfucker."

Still another side entirely of B.I.G. was his desire to appeal to the more intellectual side of his female audience, rapping as such on Big Poppa, "most of these niggaz think they be mackin but they be actin, Who they attractin with that line, 'What's your name, what's your sign?' Soon as he buy that wine, I just creep up from behind, And ask what your interests are, who you be with? Things to make you smile, what numbers to dial?"

These songs would go on to affect the urban masses, as Biggie longed with them for easier times, even as they came his way as his career began to take off. "Remember back in the days, when niggaz had waves, Gazelle shades and corn braids, Pitchin pennies, honeys had the high top jellies, Shootin skelly, motherfuckers was all friendly, Loungin at the barbeques, drinkin brews with the neighborhood crews, hangin on the avenues."

Perhaps most impressive on Biggie's debut album was his extremely developed and educated social conscience, not only as it applied to his generation, but also to his child's, "I'm seeing body after body and our mayor Guiliani, ain't tryin to see no black man turn to John Gotti, My daughter use a potty so she's older now, Educated—street knowledge, I'ma mold 'er now."

On a whole other level, Christopher Wallace confronted the despair of the young black male in vivid terms on his album in a frank dialogue with listeners everyone was hearing for the first time in hip-hop's history. While on one hand Biggie bragged requisitely about his player persona with the ladies and hustler persona with the homies, privately, he appeared in the same time to be ashamed of what his life had amounted to at such a tender age.

Because young black males culturally tend to acknowledge a life expectancy of 21, it was fitting in a strange but tangible way that Biggie would feel as hopeless within himself as he did while at the same time trying to make the ascension to hip-hop stardom. He was definitely climbing out of a personal hell of some sort when he recorded his most personally revealing track on *Ready to Die*, entitled '*Suicidal Thoughts*', in which he confesses his sins, along with a desire to end his own life, to a friend played by Sean Combs, as well as to listeners, confiding that "when I die, fuck it I wanna go to hell, Cause I'm a piece of shit, it ain't hard to fuckin' tell, Crime after crime, from drugs to extortion, I know my mother wished she got a fuckin' abortion."

Reflecting a guilt at the way he had disappointed Voletta Wallace, he continues, wondering if she would miss him if he did take his own life in the face of all he had done to disappoint her, "All my life I been considered as the worst, Lyin' to my mother, even stealin' out her purse. She don't even love me like she did when I was younger, Suckin' on her chest just to stop my fuckin' hunger, I wonder if I died, would tears come to her eyes? Forgive me for my disrespect, forgive me for my lies."

In facing the gravity of his responsibility as a father, Biggie examines the desire to take his own life in a completely different light when he weighs the guilt over potentially abandoning them to grow up in a single-parent home as he did, sarcastically rapping that "my baby's mother's 8 months, her big sister's 2, Who's to blame for both of them (naw nigga, not you)."

Ultimately, Biggie, who does take his own life in the song, was perhaps freeing himself of the guilt and responsibility, if even for a moment, or alternately might have just been describing hopelessness at its worst for the average young black male, both in terms of how he saw himself, and how he believed others viewed him... equally as worthless as he was at times within the reflection of his own self image. "I swear to God I just want to slit my wrists and end this bullshit...Throw the Magnum to my head...And squeeze, until the bed's, completely red. I'm glad I'm dead, a worthless fuckin' Buddha head."

There is no significant inference to be drawn on a broader level from this confessionary other than the fact that Wallace was clearly aware of every decision he had made in his life, along with its consequences, and his own role in each of them as they played out, which made him less a victim, and more a responsible adult as he turned 21 the same year his album was released. What struck listeners was the honesty he was willing to share with them about his own emotions as they related to the way in which he lived his life, and ultimately sought to make amends with the consequences of his actions. *Ready to Die* read more than anything else like a hustler's diary.

By the time *Ready to Die* was released, the effect of the record among consumers was just that, a release. Everything that Biggie had built up in his adolescence—the frustration, the anger, the street knowledge, and the raw ambition—all exploded in one gigantic impact that shook the foundations of East Coast hip-hop, exposing the weaknesses in its foundations, and in Biggie's own life.

On one of *Ready to Die's* most startling tracks, *Suicidal Thoughts*, Biggie worked through the culmination of the pressures in his life to the point of absolute desperation, and with no end in sight aside from the dead ones, any listener could tell that he had very really entertained the thought, based on how his life up unto that point had gone. "The situation was where I had a gun to my head and was thinking it over because I was tired of being in the mind-state of having to hustle just to feed my daughter at the time. And, just being in that mind-state selling drugs and being on the street 'cause my mother told me to get out of her house.

Everything was just looking real down. I was to the point where if I did kill myself, nobody would miss me." But plenty of people would have missed Biggie, had they, and he at the time, known what he had to offer the world as an emcee. Biggie always knew he could rap, revealing a very prominent side of his personality that translated readily as an irresistible part of his appeal as a rapper, that being his confidence.

As Lil Kim had experienced in the years prior to his sweet talking women on a national level via hits like *Big Poppa* and *One More Chance*, Biggie had his game down tight talking to women on the corners. Despite his awkward physical appearance, Biggie had no problems attracting female attention. And in discussing the latter in his rhymes, he displayed yet another distinctive personality trait…his potent sense of humor. He displayed hi humor mainly in talking self-effacingly about his looks, "I mean man, you gotta be realistic…I'm black, I'm overweight, I got a cock eye…Versace, and all that stuff…I don't wear it, I can't fit it. You'll never catch me in no Versace shit because he don't make my size. Nor Moschino, nor Donna Karan, none of that shit. They don't make that for me…I wouldn't be considered pretty, never been pretty, but what makes me pretty is my charm and my personality. I can talk to a girl and if a girl was to close her eyes she swear I was Denzel Washington."

Biggie's sense of humor was undeniably part of what endeared him to legions of rap fans, and is a part of his character that friends remember and cherish, even in his earliest and hungriest days, as an up and coming emcee. As Mark Pitts, Biggie's manager, remembers in describing Biggie's sense of humor in his early days with Bad Boy, "Big was always a funny guy, (even) when his clothing was army fatigues and dark shades. He was a clown son, he always had jokes. He had a nickname for everyone. He called me Quiet Boy first, then Gucci Don."

Biggie's sense of humor also came to play front and center in the songs on *Ready to Die*, as one critic characterized perfectly when he observed in a review of the release, that "The grim humor of B.I.G.'s lyrics emphasized the claustrophobia of his ghetto universe. On '*Warning*,' he raps, 'There's gonna be a lot of slow singing and flower bringing, if my burglar alarm starts ringing.'"

As his widow Faith Evans also recalled in the course of her first encounter with Biggie at a video shoot, regarding his unique knack for humor in the face of his ominous image. It was part of what attracted her immediately to him as a larger part of Biggie's way with words, so much so that a short twelve days later the couple would wed. "He had a certain charm about him that was very attractive. Like…he could just say the right thing, I guess…all the time. Even if he happened to do something to make you upset, you couldn't stay mad at him 'cause he was just a funny guy…He knew how to change it, especially if the heat was on him. He knew how to get out of it. I guess he had the gift of gab. He had a way with words, you know."

Biggie's way with words had helped him get off the streets and into a record deal with Sean Combs, and as 1992 continued into 1993, and the recording of '*Ready to Die*' drug on, the hip-hop womb was preparing to give birth to the overnight phenomenon of the Notorious B.I.G.

"Yeah, this album is dedicated to all the teachers that told me I'd never amount to nothin', to all the people that lived above the buildings that I was hustlin' in front of that called the police on me when I was just tryin' to make some money to feed my daughter, and all the niggaz in the struggle, you know what I'm sayin'?

Uh-ha, it's all good baby baby, ungh!"
—Biggie Smalls, *Juicy*

Chapter 6
Blowin' Up!

Upon its release, *Ready to Die* landed like an atom bomb upon, what at the time was, the East Coast's already war-torn soundscape, obliterating all the competition in one loud thump of the bass. Biggie's voice boomed like thunder out the speakers of every woofer in every SUV across New York's five boroughs, and soon thereafter, across the country. His resonance was immediate, his impact devastating in that it destroyed even the East Coast's existing styles, reinventing an entire coastal genre and blueprint for competition in the industry just the way Dr. Dre's *The Chronic* had two years earlier across the country for West Coast rap.

Rolling Stone Magazine dubbed Biggie's debut album, "*Ready to Die* is the strongest solo rap debut since Ice Cube's *Amerikkka's Most Wanted*. From the breathtakingly visual moments of his birth to his Cobainesque end in "'*Suicidal Thoughts*,' B.I.G. proves a captivating listen. It's difficult to get him out of your head once you sample what he has to offer."

Biggie personally looked at the album as his first and last shot at escaping the ghetto he had grown up in and around, telling one journalist that he was at a point personally when he recorded it that was perhaps as desperate as his everyday circumstance and surrounding. "I named (the album *Ready to Die*) 'cause it gets to a certain point in people's lives sometimes when things just be going wrong. My pops left me when I was real little and my moms worked and went to school. I don't have any brothers and sisters and I just had to do things for myself. There were times when I was dead-ass broke; mom duke wasn't giving me money, and I wasn't phuckking with niggas like that. I wasn't trying to kill myself and ready to die, but I was like ready to do whatever I had to do to get dough. Even if it involved risking my life, I just had to make it happen."

Giving the debut 4 stars, *Rolling Stone* writer Cheo Coker went on to explore Biggie's Jekyl & Hyde-esque hip-hop persona, pointing out that "B.I.G. walks along the razor's edge, hat in hand, a self-described menace to society (and sexual dynamo), yet haunted by his own propensity for heartless violence and self-destruction."

Biggie himself described *Ready to Die* as a concept album, explaining that "It's just like a big pie, with each slice indicating a different point in my life involving bitches and niggaz…from the beginning to the end. I feel I made an East Coast movie, for niggaz on both sides to recognize and respect. I'm trying to do everything. I got party records, songs for ladies, stories. I just didn't want to leave it one way, 'cause I think that's a problem to me, because if I rap a certain way I'm only gonna get money that one certain way. If everybody rapped about different things that other people can relate to, then you can get other money. It's all about money, man. You a fool if you [say] 'I'm in it for the love of Hip-Hop!' You in it for the cream, straight up and down, baby bro. 'Cause hip-Hop ain't gonna pay that car note. Hip-hop is not gonna pay the rent. The money is."

Elaborating on Biggie's lyrical abilities as a ghetto renaissance man, Coker points out that "B.I.G. maintains a consistent level of tension by juxtaposing emotional highs and lows. One minute he sits on the curb reminiscing about more innocent times when parents had more control over their kids and there weren't so many guns

'*Things Done Changed*'. The next minute, he's rapping against himself as part of a Laurel and Hardy-like stickup duo. He's the one doing dirt, boasting of a boosting career that dates back to the days of slavery '*Gimme the Loot*'. A few songs later he makes something of himself in the rap game '*Juicy*'. But soon after, in '*Everyday Struggle*,' barks of his frustration with the fast life, the lack of people he can trust and how he hears 'death knockin' at [his] front door.'"

Coker is also able to pick up, as vividly as fans, on the fact that Biggie's lyrics are like mental home movies of his urban neighborhood & its inherent strife, giving listeners a front-row view inside the mind of a hustler from a grittier, more authentic point of view than it had been up to that point. Most notably for a rap critic, Coker notes "With his prodigious, often booming voice overwhelming the track, Biggie sweeps his verbal camera high and low, painting a sonic picture so vibrant that you're transported right to the scene. He raps in clear, sparse terms, allowing the lyrics to hit the first time you hear them."

While Biggie covered arguably every conceivable aspect of the hustler lifestyle and persona on his first LP, the most riveting was his discussion of the despair and hopelessness of the inner city, and its toll on the hustler and his family, in the context of Wallace's desire to give up and end his own life. '*Suicidal Thoughts*' was the album's most personal and poignant track, and the first time in hip-hop's history that a platinum MC had openly discussed the prospect, or admitted that he thought about it for that matter. It displayed a human weakness, a vulnerability in the hardened outward persona of the hustler, and for that matter, of the young, black male that America-at-large had not been exposed to prior thereto.

Biggie opened up candidly about the song and album title in interview after interview surrounding the release of *Ready to Die*, explaining quite literally that "I had the gun to my head and was thinking it over because I was tired of being in the mind-state of having to hustle just to feed my daughter at the time. And just being in that mind-state selling drugs and just being in the street 'cause my mother told me to get out her house. Everything was just looking real down. I was to the point where if I did kill myself, nobody would miss me. That was the ideal behind *Suicidal thoughts.*"

Delving further into the psychology behind the song, Biggie explained that he felt that it wasn't that unique for a young, black male from the inner city to be speaking so candidly about suicide as an option, rather just for a rapper, which is why it sounded so profound. On another level, while Biggie was ready to acknowledge that he had contemplated the act himself in the past, he was not ready as a role model to take responsibility for causing anyone else to consider it in the future tense, "I mean, shit like (*Suicidal Thoughts*) could torment a nigga and fuck his head up…A nigga that's really stressed out might hear that shit and might flip, and I really can't handle that. I don't want to be the cause of someone hurting themselves, but I'm just trying to keep it as real as possible."

His goal with the song seemed to be to represent the bleakness of the inner city through the song in terms of the affects on its people. To Biggie, America was already aware of the requisite plights of his neighborhood—poverty, drug dealing and addiction, gang violence, and so forth. What the public-at-large had not done however, was to process the affects of these adversities personally for themselves, so that they then might feel some of the responsibility for its existence personally, rather than continue to turn a blind eye.

Only fellow MC Ice Cube had attempted this sort of exposure on his debut LP *America's Most Wanted* on the underground classic '*The Nigga Ya Love ta Hate*', where he had warned 'It ain't wise to chastise and preach, just open the eyes of each.' Biggie wasn't preaching, rather just stating the obvious from one populations' experience and perspective where another just across a poverty line in the middle and upper class remained oblivious by choice, pre-ferring to be uninformed and ignorant to a societal problem that could no longer be ignored.

The gravity of Biggie's own hopeless would soon be felt on a platinum level, as rap was more and more becoming the inner city's bully pulpit in place of the corporate media. Wallace may have become a superstar, but he displayed a very real awareness that he was no more special than the next African American in terms of what his people were still going through on a daily basis. More importantly, Biggie seemed to point out through the song that, at times, the only shelter he felt amidst the everyday bleakness of his world was the very blanket of hopelessness that covered it, in that things couldn't get any darker, and that suicide was therein a potential source of protection or relief from it all.

If Biggie, given his talent, had, at any time, been pushed to the point where he had felt suicide was his only option, then helplessness itself had been pushed to a new extreme, and America needed to listen up more than ever—especially as their children were beginning to. "I know it goes through everybody's mind, man. 'Cause if it went through mine, it's going to go through everybody's else's, 'cause I'm no different from no nigga on the street. So, I just wrote about it. I put all the stresses of like, 'My baby's mom is eight months and her little sister's two, and they're both my kids.'"

In the end, '*Suicidal Thoughts*' was emblematic of a larger theme within the album-wide context of Biggie's mind-state at the time the record was released ...one in which he saw he had a shot at something, but didn't know what or how big. From that vantage point, the lyrical content is so expansive in subject matter, variety, depth and honesty because Wallace clearly thought it might be his first, last, and only opportunity to represent to the fullest, and so he did.

Even more importantly, to Wallace was the fact that he had already reached the point of not giving a fuck in his personal life to where he was desensitized enough; and because of his surroundings could speak completely freely on any subject without considering the consequence. This proved him a power and resonance he couldn't have been aware of beforehand. "Basically with a first album…on songs like those, you hear a lot of anger. Here was this stressed Black boy who got him a record deal and got a whole lot of shit to talk about. "When I did *Ready to Die*, I felt like I was already dead. I felt like my soul was already dead and I was just releasing a lot of energy."

Still, in spite of the dark, dismal depression hanging over him personally, Biggie was also able to conjure an impressive resolve professionally. Enough so, to get motivated through the recording and release of his debut album to graduate emotionally, and to have both hope and excitement at the prospect of getting himself, his family and his crew out of the circumstances he rapped so vividly about on the record for good. "My album dropped Friday the 13th while I was on the road and niggaz was betting on how much I was sellin' per week! I sold damn near a quarter of a million records in NY, dog! That's damn near impossible! Nothin' is gonna stop me from lettin' me or my family eat!"

Perhaps more importantly from a social perspective beyond his immediate loved ones, Biggie also had plans for his audience, specifically in getting the word out on their behalf, wherein he was happy to share in the spotlight, "That's not just me, I guess that's why my music is so heartfelt. There's a lotta niggas that going through the same situation just like me. You know what I'm sayin'?"

With his lyrical arsenal and enemies mentally mapped out, Biggie set out recording *Ready to Die* with an open mind, musically speaking. He was free to do so because of the confidence he had in his rhymes. Upon impact, while even Biggie was surprised at the platinum reception, he expected it to a degree, based on having his own ass as an MC covered. "I knew, lyrically the shit was tight. And I knew that no other album was really coming like that, but I didn't know it was going to blow up and become the album for the 90s. I just knew that it was put together properly."

The recording of *Ready to Die* was a pressured time for everyone around Biggie, as well, as it was Sean 'P. Diddy' Combs' debut release off Bad Boy Entertainment—his new joint-venture label with Arista. Combs had signed a $10 million deal a year earlier in 1992 with Clive Davis, and knew this album would either launch him into the stratosphere as an entrepreneur along with his marquee rapper, or would cause him a major setback in his own quest to become a mogul.

Combs certainly had Biggie's creative confidence, as he validated in one interview following the record's release and success. Such that, while Combs gave Smalls complete lyrical freedom, Biggie reciprocated musically, acknowledging readily that he was still very much a student in the studio. "Lyrically, (I controlled) everything. Production wise, I didn't make any beats. I had my choice of beats. Easy Mo B. would give me a tape with about 20 beats and I'd pick the one that I'd liked and rap to it. And Puffy would pick out certain beats and say rap to this joint right here or that beat is tight rap to that right here; and if I like it, I would...I mean, Puff, he gives me beats, but he don't like say, 'You gotta rhyme to this,' He says, 'Yo, if you went with this joint right here, you're outta here.'"

Elaborating further, Smalls explained how their collaborative process worked on specific singles that went onto become chart smashes, offering more insight into the close relationship he shared on a professional and personal level with Combs, amplified by the mutual respect they had for one another. "That's what he said on 'Big Poppa'. He said, 'Yo, dog, your voice over this beat right here, you're gone. I mean it's definitely a gold single.' And I'm listenin' to the beat. I always loved it. I loved it when Q-Tip flipped it with the 'Bonita Applebum' remix joint. So I was like, 'Yo, I'm with it. I don't give a fuck.' I mean, that nigga track record is like 99%. You never gonna hear 'bout nothin' that Puff did was wack or ain't sell no records. So I kinda respect his vision and I respect his opinion. And the shit is blowin' up crazy, so I can't even be mad at him."

Combs', while clearly on a quest to build his own resume as a producer, was also smart enough in recognizing B.I.G.'s versatility as a lyricist to know when to step back and turn the reigns over to an equally as varied number of producers stylistically to make the album as musically dynamic and diverse, and therein appealing to consumers, as possible. Combs also explained from his own perspective, as a producer and A&R man, how he went about walking the fine line between respecting Biggie's artistry and authenticity, while at the same time doing what he was necessary to make the record as accessible as possible to listeners.

"(Big) would be saying something to be trying to get his point across as far as rap wise, just trying to relate one thing to another and, it could have come across in a negative way. Like he said, one time, he said, he was talking about how he had a song on his first album called 'Gimme the Loot' and he was talking about how he just...he went in...he had to rob somebody in order to survive...in order to eat, at that point.

But, at the same time there was a story to him that was just entertainment. But, then there was one line in there that said, 'I don't care that your pregnant, gimme the baby rings and the number 1 mom pendant.' I was like, you got to say that in a different way, that's just, you know what I'm saying? You have to care if somebody's pregnant and I try my best to do that as much. But, even I have to be accountable that maybe I should have done it more. And I have to, I have to be accountable for that."

Biggie responded positively to this approach, clearly appreciative of the number of options he had in terms of backing tracks to accompany his topical variety on a lyrical level. "Easy Mo Bee is a funny nigga, man. I like him, 'cause he…if you look at him…you would not think that nigga is jam-packed with so much muthafuckin' flavor. Mo got some shit for a niggaz' ass. The Blues Brothers are dope too, man. Lord Finesse got some butter shit."

Additionally, Biggie was instinctively sharp enough to know when to step back on the marketing end and defer to Combs' expertise in choosing a single, understanding that while a rawer track like '*Machine Gun Funk*', Smalls' first choice for a debut single, would naturally pigeon-hole him as a gangster-rapper, limiting his appeal at radio, and therein, to a potentially broader fan-base.

Biggie clearly sought the latter, both in terms of his desire to get the message of his people out to the deaf masses, but also as it related to his desire to be viewed through as many perceptions as possible simultaneously, on a critical and commercial level, i.e. to become hip-hop's first Bugsy Segal, a gangster who was also a visionary and the smoothest with the ladies. "(originally), I wanted to come out with a little harder edge, but Puffy convinced me that *Juicy* kinda explains your story; it's a radio-friendly joint with the Mtume loop and it kinda like introduces the world to Biggie."

That faith paid off as Biggie began to feel the impact everyone else around him was getting from his own buzz, displaying a general attitude of optimism that stood in stark contrast to the dark, pessimism that ran rampant through the depths of his debut album just a few months earlier. He was making personal progress.

Biggie began to see the breadth of his potential once *Ready to Die* took off at retail, following Combs' lead in making plans for the future that took him above and beyond the immediate realm of hip-hop onto other lucrative, and perhaps in the long-term more stable, ventures, which he elaborated on excitedly to one journalist in a 1994 interview. "I got some shit comin' this year, no doubt! I got my own clothing line called Big Man Clothes. That's gonna be the bomb! I'm gonna drop another album that's gonna be even bigger than me! The main thing I'm gonna do is get a lump of some of lucci and start fuckin' with some real estate."

Biggie also indulged his status as a player, making sure to let his home town of New York, as well as the rest of the watching world, know who the new pimp on the block was, staying in the finest hotels, rolling in the hottest rides, and macking the hottest honeys. "On the road to the riches and diamond rings, we've been all over town, layed up in the hottest cars, rollin' three thick playin' highball with guns, girls and gangsters...Le Montrose hotel in L.A. If it ain't there, then it would probably be the Macklowe on 54th Street in Manhattan -suite 15B; that one has the view."

Like any young superstar new to the game, Biggie was living it up, sowing his royal oats, making a name for himself among peers and players. He and Combs' were building a dream together—Smalls' his career, Combs' his empire, and things couldn't have been going better as the spring of 1995 rolled around.

Still, as the new year unfolded, Biggie lived up to his reputation as one of hip-hop's hottest hustlers, switching up his flow as dynamically as he had on record, to wed his Bad Boy label-mate, R&B singer Faith Evans. Biggie was beginning to settle into the role of family man in a more normal setting than Bedford-Stuyvesant could offer. He began to sample the fruits of his success, particularly in the area of fine dining, one which Biggie was naturally as equipped for as rapping, and one in which he had no problem indulging. "I like Italian food, but I be eatin' everywhere. I'm an average man. I'll go to the corner store and get me a hero if that's what I feel like eatin'. My wife know a spot right over the bridge that serves good Italian food right off Canal St. Other than that, Faith'll cook up some baked ziti or something. You know she got skills. She's with me."

Biggie also doted on his baby girl, now 3, indulging her wherever he could with his newfound success. "My daughter...I want to have my shit together so that she'll have her life together. I wanna give anything and everything possible. Whatever she wants." As a parent, Biggie sought to provide a better material upbringing for his daughter than he, himself, had experienced. The rapper also displayed an active consciousness about the possible influence his music could have on his daughter, which he discussed candidly in interviews.

Additionally, he articulated an awareness concerning the responsibility he had to both physically protect her from the world he was discussing in his music, while at the same time making his child aware of his own roots, so she could appreciate what she herself was growing up around in place of it. It was a fine line to walk, which Biggie seemed, like everything else, to do almost masterfully. "I'm in a stage right now where my daughter's three years old; all she knows is 'Big Poppa' and '*One More Chance*'—the new single—and that Daddy's on TV. That's it…She wouldn't understand the harder stuff. All she's into is what's on the video. And by the time she gets to the age where she can understand everything, I'm sure I'll let her listen to those records and explain everything that happened in my life."

Still, despite the bling-bling and upgrade in his own lifestyle, Biggie still attempted to stay on point with his message to younger fans watching him for cues on how they themselves could make the jump from the street corner to the stage. His biggest piece of advice seemed to be to have the confidence of a superstar, even as a nobody, be unafraid to take whatever chance you have to toward the end of making it, but never to forget where you are coming from along the way.

Biggie, at least in part, put his player lifestyle on display once he had it so that others could use it as an example of how to dream…knowing it could come true. At the same time, he put his wealth on wax in '*Juicy*' well before he really had any to drive that very same point home. "Any number can be played, but you gotta play for keeps. G-Men ain't afraid of beef. The suckers list consists of bullshit niggaz who are scared to take big risks, but want the big reward. Usually these are the ones who sit and wait for things to happen instead of makin' shit happen. We've all made our bones one way or another. Bit it's a Smalls' world to see a New York G from Tuph St. graduate from Platinum High School. Real niggaz know when to quit and pick on the new shit. To be or not to be ain't the question, it's what you'll become that matters. Yeah, it's nice to have fat shit. the Versace, the Rolex, the whole nine, but there's one more thing that not to be forgotten—you got to start small if you're ever to become B.I.G. Why?! 'Cause I knew I was gonna get it. Kids who like my shit know that it ain't beyond their reach. I showed them they could have all that good shit if they (really) try."

Along the way to achieving any dream, Biggie dispensed perhaps his most chilling but grounded piece of advice to hustlers seeking to make it. He warned them to watch out for player-haters, and to dream with eyes wide open rather than shut to the immediate realities of the inner city he had escaped from. He drove the latter point home by illustrating his own uncertainty in how long he would really last in the game…despite his ambition to become a legend…or his platinum success, thus far toward that end.

In a very real way, Smalls could never truly realize his dream of completely escaping the dangers of his background, because lived in an almost constant state of paranoia, looking over his shoulder even as he tried to look ahead to the future. "Sometimes, I can't really picture (what my life will be like in 10 years). I ain't gonna lie to you. I never even pictured being like even 35. I guess 'cause (I'm) always living day to day, and, there's always so many things that could just (snuff) me out. The way niggaz be trippin' out here, I really can't plan; shit be going wrong anyway. We just living day to day. We know what we wanna do, but we don't know how long it's gonna take."

Frank White…I been with my nigga before he came in the game
No one's, no V's, we used to take the train…
But he was my nigga, and I was his bitch
I rolled hard with him, how could I forget
Had beef with yo wife that ain't patched up
But still got love for your kids…
If I'm fucked up, imagine how Mrs. Wallace feels
Sometimes I sit and think how it would be if we was married
Of if I woulda kept the child that I carried…
We miss you so much, I love you so much
Never thought life without you would be so rough…
This is somethin' young kids just won't understand
How they took away this beautiful man…
It's been hard, but I told God that I put up a fight
So here's a Long Kiss Goodnight, Frank White

—Kimberly Jones a.k.a. Lil Kim

Chapter 7
No Ordinary Love—
Christopher Wallace and
Kimberly Jones

Looking inside of love forbidden, the soul of true devotion more often than not is hidden, naked, baring itself only for shadows and hiding from the world's disapproving eye. With eyes closed, the fantastical often becomes the possible, chastity becomes open, and hearts beat freely—arguably because the subconscious is blind to consequence. In both her rhyme and commercial demeanor, hip-hop diva Lil Kim has distinguished herself as a ghetto-fabulous illustration of not just the happy, but erotic medium that blooms out of an amalgamation of an intriguingly raw, sexual energy and an intimate understanding of that sexual power as a channel capable of capturing and controlling the mass erection of hip-hop record buyers who came in droves to Kim's erotic and tantalizing lyrical invitation.

Her mentor in the latter discipline—Big Poppa, the Notorious B.I.G. When listening to Lil Kim, on stage, in a video, or on record, one can't help but envision the image of her sucking playfully on a lollipop, toying the candy ball salaciously with her tongue, much in the way she lyrically toys with our minds, whether on the periphery of a societally-repressed eroticism, or in explicit, hard core terms for more seasoned listeners.

In metaphorical terms, Kim played the part of Jodie Foster in Taxi Driver, Notorious BIG playing the role of Harvey Kietel's pimp. While on the streets or on record, talking to horny men or to horny record buyers, Kim, like Foster, appeared the cultured virgin, a metaphorical title, with an entire undertone, another level of sexual nuance begging to be explored. A world so hot it even made Kim horny, though she had explored that ocean floor a million times over, it still felt like the first time every time. She was that hot. Kim commercially was an immediate intrigue to anyone. She held nothing and everything back in the same time, made reality of what was very much fantasy.

Kim was very much a performer in this respect, exemplifying an extraordinary ability to be as universally appealing sexually as a prostitute might, when in reality her experience in the latter discipline was limited very much to one man. Kim's confidence as hip-hop's public lover was drawn very much from her teacher. The man who had played a fundamental role in helping her transition from a teenager into womanhood, to become comfortable enough with her sexuality privately to utilize it as a commercial tool in transforming herself into a solo artist. Because Kim trusted privately in Biggie as implicitly as she is, she seemed publicly able to make herself as sexually accessible as her image was. She always had his arms to fall back into, remarking once, that "Biggie…always sheltered me. I like a protector. Fathers don't let nothing happen to their baby girl."

Kimberly Jones loved Christopher Wallace with her eyes very much open, where the rest of the world would shake its collective head in disapproval, and largely in denial, of a reciprocal passion that was both primal and potent. Therein lay the root of both its endurance and antagonism. While Christopher Wallace, as the Notorious B.I.G., would leave Kim to marry another woman,

Faith Evans, who would give birth to his son, Wallace's subsequent divorce from Evans would give way to a rekindled romance with Kim that took on a more mature tone from the couple's earlier days. It is in this period shortly preceding B.I.G.'s demise, that Kim would begin to see the path Wallace desired his life to follow…a more calm existence…which, very possibly could have centered around the resilience of the love between Wallace and Kim.

Even as a homeless sixteen-year-old living largely on the streets of Bedford Stuyvesant, when Kimberly Jones first met Christopher Wallace, who was then still a street hustler, the role he took on with her was one of a mentor…only the game back then was survival. Though the relationship would flourish into the creative when Biggie blew up as an MC and made Kimberly Jones part of his crew, Junior Mafia, their union began as something much rawer, wherein Kim was an unpolished diamond that Christopher took quickly to shining. Kim, in reflecting back, clearly views herself as Biggie's protégé, with Wallace as someone who "was like a father figure and husband…to me."

To prove Biggie's motives pure of ulterior agendas, he was involved with Kim long before he knew of her potential as an MC, and was protective of her more in that time as a raw companion than as an artist. In turn, Kim fell in love with everything Christopher was as a person, from "the way he danced (to the way he walked, (and) the way he talked", as she recalled to Ebony Magazine in an exclusive interview October 2000.

Though their chameleon chemistry would work magic on tape, as well as on the street, to truly explore its essence, one must begin back on the streets of Bed Stuy in Brooklyn, New York. As Kim herself remembers, Biggie's first efforts toward promoting her as an MC may have been based more on his affections for her than immediate faith in her potential as a star, "We lived on the same block in Brooklyn. I always thought he was cute, and when I first started talking to him, I felt like I'd known him for years…I was working at Bloomingdale's, and friends of mine said to him, 'You know, Kim knows how to rap.' He was like 'Please! She's too cute to know how to rap.' Then I just happened to pass him on the street, and he said 'Kim, I heard you can rap!' I blushed, and he said 'You don't know how to rap!' He was a very good manipulator. He could get you to do anything he wanted. So I said, 'Yes I do', and I started rhyming. He knew that I needed work…Biggie thought I was just going to be this little female in the back (of the Junior Mafa), this girl he'd put in the group because he loved me."

To that end, love was clearly the bedrock of the relationship between Kim and Biggie, though the media has often sought to paint Kim more as Biggie's plaything than as any sort of a legitimate romantic interest. In fact, at the height of Biggie's popularity, the hip-hop media painted Lil Kim as his very public mistress, pitting him in between Kim and wife and fellow Bad Boy Entertainment artist Faith Evans, whom Biggie had met at a video shoot and married following a 12-day, whirlwind romance. Kim herself did little to downplay this characterization. At one point, in an interview following the rapper's slaying, even going so far as to agree with the latter characterization, but reasoning that she would have taken him any way she could have had him, such that "I wanted to be with him, and he knew that it couldn't happen. That was my heart…my mentor, my boy. And you're absolutely right, I was a Mistress. But I hated the fact that that is what I stood for…I put him before Him, you know?"

As Biggie described the relationship, as it developed, both professionally and personally, he was clearly torn between Kim and Faith, and ultimately had to make a choice. "Kim was like what you would call an amateur and I made her a professional, lyrically. Not like business wise or nothing like that. I just wanted to school my artists the way Puffy schooled me.

(We were lovers for a while.) That's still my partner though. I still love her. [pause] You ever saw Good Fellas?..You know the part in Good Fellas when Henry got married and everything, and he was in love with his wife but at the same time he had a girlfriend on the side? And it was gettin' to the point where his wife was gettin' real hysterical; and Pauly and Jimmy had to come see him and tell him, Listen you got a wife and a family and you gotta go home?…Well, that's the situation that I had gotten myself in….I had to go home. I couldn't be wild all the time."

Though for a while, Biggie and Faith would be courted by the press as the Prince and Princess of hardcore East Coast hip-hop, Kim always managed to maintain a visible role just off to their side. In interviews where journalists broached the subject, Kim often sought to play down the depth of the union, remarking that "(Biggie) was fascinated with light-skinned women. He always wanted that. And when he became 'Big Poppa', he was able to get all of that."

Still, despite her antagonist attitude toward Biggie's new bride, Kim would in the same breath readily admit that the union had crushed her, as "Biggie was my everything. He was someone that I loved very dearly. He and I were soul mates." Every interview with Biggie made mention of his relationship with Kim, in some instances even suggesting that the two were involved while Biggie was still married to Evans. Kim never worked to dispute that their relationship was an ongoing thing, as it very much was. As Kim professed to one inquiry regarding her potential for ever loving another man the way she did Christopher Wallace. "Never (would I love anyone again the way I loved Biggie)! Biggie's the only person I will ever love and have ever loved, period."

No matter how anyone looking at his life does so, objectively or scrupulously, Biggie was loved. Whether primal, maternal, instantaneous, concerning his legions of adoring fans, or via a more earned love rooted in respect, as was in the case of Sean "Puffy"

Combs, Christopher Wallace was treasured. Kim, better than anyone, understood this from the perspective of scheming females, reasoning that "I can't blame a woman for wanting to be with him. He loved women. He was a very charming man."

And while many women may be able to lay some claim to Biggie's heart, very few can call themselves his true companion the way Kim can. This is based partially on the fact that their relationship embodied a resilience that transcended celebrity and the implied distractions, centering in on something much more tangible in the sense of the long term. In Kim's eyes, she saw Biggie's marriage to Evans as another phase, and one which would pass, as she and Biggie would have eventually been together no matter what the adversity, simply, because "he was close to my heart…If he were here today, I think we would be really close. We wouldn't be married. But I think as the years went on, we would have gotten married. Being with him always made me happy."

Kim's faith in her adoring disposition toward Biggie stood in contrast to considerable adversity in the course of Christopher Wallace's brief but phenomenal life as a hip-hop superstar, wherein the horror-or-highlight reel (depending on your perspective), included Wallace's marriage to Evans, and a decision on the part of Wallace and Kim to abort a child she had conceived with the rapper shortly before his death in 1997, a decision Kim maintains they made jointly, on Wallace's part out of concern for how the birth would affect her career, and on Kim's part, as she recalls, "(on one hand) I wanted to have it. He was very supportive. But he knew I wanted this career more than anything, and he knew that I wasn't going to have the baby."

Still, despite the abortion, Kim saw the resilience of her relationship with Biggie coming full circle shortly before they were robbed of a chance to realize that destiny when Wallace was murdered in 1997. As she remembered, all the signs were there between the two, such that "just before he passed I saw that we had a future.

Two weeks before he died, I spoke to him, and he said things he never would have said to me before. He said 'I love you so much and we're going to be together sooner than you think.' And he said it repeatedly. To Biggie, once was enough—he was so macho. So, I knew that there was a future."

Part of what seemed to resonate most clearly with Kim in Biggie's revelation was the honesty he shared with her, in admitting he had been wrong to leave her. Wallace, as Kim remembered, had opened himself fully to her, which only a complete understanding with someone typically allows. "(Biggie) said, 'I want to make peace between us, because I know I hurt you. You are a beautiful person inside and out, and I felt like sometimes I didn't deserve you, and you deserve better.' I said 'OK, I love you and I'll be there for you.'"

Biggie himself had discussed his desire to settle down shortly before his death, and following his divorce from Faith Evans; and in doing so, detailed a vision that was a far cry from his beginnings as a hustler on St. James Avenue in Brooklyn, wherein "when I set myself down…I was like 'Yo Big, this hustling shit is for the birds. I could fuck around and get murdered out in these streets', and decided so step up my shit. I wasn't thinking, 'One day I'm gonna get rich and still live in the hood.' My dream house has a picket fence and green grass. I picture my daughter playin' out in my backyard on the swing and on the jungle gyms. Ain't none of that shit poppin' off in Brooklyn."

While the question of whether Kim, in retrospect, feels she was cheated out of her chance at a lifetime commitment with Biggie or not, remains to be answered, she clearly has chosen to view his death as a test of her will to go on living, with or without the man she chose as the love of her life. As Kim reasoned, "I used to say, 'I can't live without this man.' I know God was like, 'Alright, watch this.' God does this to see how much you appreciate him." Following in the bittersweet vein of the religious doctrine that God giveth and God taketh away, Kim appears to have strived within herself to come to terms with why God took Biggie from her. Part of her reckoning has come via a broader understanding of why she feels Biggie was put in the position he was placed in as a Hip-hop sensation in the first place, for as his style opened many new doors for up and coming MCs, it ultimately closed his own prematurely.

Kim seems to find perspective in an understanding that, while she inevitably had to share Biggie with the rest of the world for the sake of his talent as it related to the betterment of hip-hop, she had him first. Those roots are what she has held onto in working through the loss of her best friend, mentor, and lover, likening herself and Biggie to the equivalent of "Bonnie and Clyde for real…we were really partners…And we lived our lives like that…He taught me everything I know…Biggie is still the greatest rapper in the world. That's why God put him in this world, so that everybody could get a taste of what this game is all about."

Ironically, Biggie began parlaying his game as an MC almost by accident, while he was still working full time as a crack dealer on Bushwick Avenue. From the outset, Biggie had no illusions about his available opportunities in life as a young, African American male coming out of the projects with no high school diploma and a daughter to feed. On paper, Christopher Wallace was, coming up in the game, very much a stereotype, a few digits among a massive and ugly statistic that served to institutionally disadvantage minorities who came up in impoverished neighborhoods like Biggie's.

As the rapper recalled on his accidental happening into rap early on, "I was a full-time 100 percent hustler. Sellin' drugs, waking up early in the morning, hitting the set selling my shit 'til the crack of dawn. My mother goin' to work would see me out there in the morning. That's how I was on it…I used to hang out with the OGB Crew, the Old Gold Brothers, over on Bedford Ave…It was fun just hearing myself on tape over the beats…It was just something I always did for fun as far back as I can remember…I (never) planned for it to be a career. It started by accident…doing some tapes in a basement."

Another forgotten statistic, Lil Kim, back in her days as sixteen-year-old Kimberly Jones, remembers being around as another kid on the block when Biggie was still a hustler coming up, "I always loved music…and when Biggie found out I could rhyme he helped put me on." As part of Biggie's crew, Junior Mafia, Kim enjoyed being under both Biggie's professional and personal wing, "He taught me everything I know, so how could I not give him props for making my album blazing."

Still as Junior Mafia began to take off on the wings of Biggie's own success, hits such as *Player's Anthem*, signaled to Biggie that Kim held something special as an MC that made her a standout in the group, holding potential for superstardom in her own right. To that end, when Biggie encouraged Kim to go solo, she took the advice on the condition that Biggie would be there with her every step along the way. That included putting together her debut album, *Hardcore*, which Biggie helped produce and released under his own independent label, Undertainment Records, via Atlantic Records.

As Kim recalls the recording process, it was one of collaboration between Biggie and her that served to add another branch to their already blooming relationship, "Biggie was growing as a producer. When he was putting my album together, he knew what he wanted me to do. He'd go, 'I want you to write to this beat.' Biggie was a beautiful poet. He was like Langston Hughes…Biggie and I basically had the same mind, the same ear, the same ideas. He helped me the first time, so that means he's still helping me." Unfortunately, some critics within the hip-hop media didn't take Kim seriously as a solo artist when her first album, *Hard Core*, was released in 1996.

While the content of the album served in part to reveal the closeness she and B.I.G. shared, as he had served among other things, as the album's executive producer, the attention the critics paid to Biggie's involvement in some ways worked to hurt Kim's initial credibility. To a host of charges that have been lodged against Kim concerning the extent of B.I.G.'s involvement in producing her album, specifically as that involvement related to the writing of the album's lyrical content, Kim has tried to respond in a measured manner which both maintained the integrity and beauty of the work that she and Biggie did achieve together through the collaboration. But, in the same time it served to protect Kim's individual accomplishment and growth as a solo artist in the course of the album's production, something she feels Biggie clearly would have wanted.

In clearing up the fact from the fiction within the allegations, Kim has pointed out that while "a lot of people always assumed that Biggie wrote for me…yeah, he helped me out a lot, but I wrote all my music, I wrote everything. He may have written a few verses on my first album, but I'm gonna let you know right now, he was the only one that I would let do that for me…There were a lot of people telling me what to do…But I was also being myself, and that shines through."

Sadly, Biggie's slaying in many ways forced Kim to take her professional direction to the next level. Partially, she has reasoned, because it is a transition Biggie would have wanted her to make either way, such that "After he died, honestly, I wanted to remain a baby for a while. His death forced me to become mature too soon. And he was everything to me. My father, sister, brother. He would tell me when to go to sleep, when to wake up. It was crazy. So I wasn't very confident…I was depressed, very scared and nervous. Biggie had always been there to tell me what to do."

Part of moving on entailed facing the part of herself that was so dependant on Biggie, and exploring ways to mature from that place into full-blown womanhood as a female and artist. Clearly, Christopher Wallace's departure from her life has not been an easy thing to accept, artistically or personally, and Kim has not sought to entirely let go of it. The anger seems to work as something of a motivation for her toward resolving both what her role ultimately was in B.I.G.'s life, and what her role as an artist and female hip-hop icon ultimately will be in a historical light.

As Kim has described the latter personal/ professional conflict as the two worlds naturally seem to ever-intertwine, she distinguishes the two with a unified point she hopes to be in at one point in her life, a place where she won't have B.I.G, but possibly the peace he sought ultimately for himself and whoever his partner in life would ultimately have been.

Kim's more recent material, boldly expressed on her most recent album, Notorious K.I.M., has sought to be a step thematically in that direction, "I got a lot to conquer. I ain't at peace. When I get at peace, y'all gon' know…I have to live, that's all. Mature. Just like B.I.G. said, if he was to sit up there and talk about robbin' and stealin' like he did on his first album, he'd be playin' himself. Well, I ain't got to fuck for car keys and double digit figures, you know what I'm sayin'? I got to go somewhere else now. I have to let it…I have to live. I just have to live."

Kim's struggle to move forward, as an individual, and an artist, in the wake of B.I.G.'s passing has not been an easy task. As she remarked to one journalist shortly following his death concerning the challenge of getting onto the next phase, let alone through the next day, "Trust me, after Biggie died, the drama did not stop…I just try to deal with it and hope that it turns out ok."

Part of Kim's challenge in moving on from B.I.G. involved coming full circle with herself sexually as an artist without B.I.G. as a critic and collaborator to fall back on. Kim seems to have achieved the latter through a great deal of soul searching, and in doing so, focused the breadth of her new material on the inner-workings of that journey, conceding readily that "I'm a very sexual person… and what I'm revealing on my album is my personality and experiences."

Those experiences, namely including the death of Christopher Wallace, have made Kim creatively and spiritually a stronger individual and artist, and in the vein that Biggie strived to become the *King of New York*, has motivated Kim to attempt to join him on the throne as the city's Queen, where, in honor of his memory, "I really want to work on becoming an icon in the (new Millennium). Some people might say I'm one now. Me, myself, I know what it takes to be an even bigger icon, and that's what I really want to do. You can't just become Diana Ross over four years, you know? You have to work at it, and then when you get it, you have to fill the need and stay that icon. Rapping is all about claiming your spot and letting everyone know you are number one at this…And nobody is taking my spot any time soon. People call me a diva, but…I'm not always real nice, but I am nice to my fans because they have nothing to do with what I'm going through."

It seems one of the most intimate elements of Kim's identity struggle has centered around filling the space B.I.G. filled as a source of support, which Kim has found in her religious faith, such that "religion is number one in my life. I may not do everything right. I'm not perfect. I'm going to fuck up…When you create a certain lifestyle, you have to keep that up in order to survive in this industry…And a lot of times, I have to go where they are. There are some things that I have to make decisions on (now) that I don't know if they are the right things, but (God) will direct me." In reflecting on whether her faith will eventually reconnect her with the love of her life, Kim seems sure in her heart that destiny will look kindly on her with respect to Christopher Wallace's place in her fate, such that "when I get to heaven, I will be with Biggie."

Biggie: (How ya livin Biggie Smalls?) I'm surrounded by criminals
Heavy rollers even the shiesty individuals
Smokin skunk and mad Phillies
Beatin down Billy Badasses, cracks in stacks and masses
If robbery's a class, bet I pass it
Shit get drastic, I'm buryin ya bastards
Big Poppa never softenin
Take you to the church, rob the preacher for the offerin
Leave the fucker coughin up blood, and his pockets like rabbit ears
Covered the wife, Kleenex for the kid's tears
Versace wear, Moschino on my bitches
She whippin my ride, countin my one's, thinkin I'm richest
Just the way players play, all day everyday
I don't know what else to say
I've been robbin niggaz since Run and them was singin 'Here We Go'
Snatchin ropes at the Roxie homeboy you didn't know
my flow, detrimental to your health
Usually roll for self, I have son ridin shotgun
My mind's my nine, my pen's my Mac-10
My target, all you wack niggaz who started rappin
Junior M.A.F.I.A. steelo, niggaz know the half
Caviar for breakfast, champagne bubble baths
Runnin up in pretty bitches constantly
The Smalls bitch, who the fuck it was supposed to be?

Chorus: So (Niggaz) Grab your dick if you love hip-hop
(Bitches) Rub your titties if you love Big Poppa
Gotcha, open off the words I say because
"This type of shit it happens everyday"

—Player's Anthem, Junior Mafia

Chapter 8

Player's Anthem:
The Junior Mafia

Biggie Smalls loyalty from his old Bedford Stuyvesant neighborhood didn't only extend to Lil Kim, once he blew up. In fact, Biggie extended the invitation to all the members of his neighborhood crew to join him in the spotlight, forming the Junior Mafia, which consisted of four separate acts: the 6s (Little Caesar, Chico and Nino Brown), the Snakes (cousins Larceny and Trife), MC Klepto, and Lil Kim.

By 1995 in hip-hop, it had become commonplace for a marquee rap act like Biggie to put his posse on following his own initial success—Ice Cube had done it with the Lynch Mob, Ice T with the Rhyme Syndicate, Snoop Dogg with the Dogg Pound, Tupac with the Outlawz. None of the crews were usually ever as remotely talented as their leader, but because of the street code of a hustler never forgetting his roots, the crew album usually served as a celebration of sorts for the fact that not only had the star rapper made it, but that he had stayed loyal to the block in bringing his boys along.

Rappers like Tupac and Ice Cube were usually featured in almost every song on the crew album, typically in the chorus or verse, or sometimes in both if it was a single, and most crew albums were expected to go gold, selling 500,000 copies. Additionally, most were released within range of the star rapper's initial blow-up in popularity to provide maximum exposure, and capitalize on the lead MC's success in selling his crew.

Most industry insiders will acknowledge privately, out of earshot of the superstar MC, that without his support, the crew would never have had a prayer on their own of getting even a development or production deal. Nevertheless, as the trend had become more of a norm, its commonplace had been developed at the promotional level into something of a formula, where the album was driven by a lead single featuring the marquee rapper prominently, usually supported by a video which introduced all the crew members individually flashing money, driving in expensive automobiles, and wearing the requisite diamond-studded label chain of whatever record label they were signed to.

In the time since Biggie introduced the world to the Junior Mafia, almost every major rap phenomenon has followed suit with their own crew—50 Cent with G Unit, Eminem with D 12, Nelly with the Saint Lunatics, Cam'ron with the Diplomats, Jay Z with Memphis Bleek, Beanie Segal, and Freeway, among others. Its a reverse in formula from the days in the late 80s and early 90s when rap groups like N.W.A., The Ghetto Boys Wu-Tang Clan, and Digital Underground were used as promotional vehicles to introduce the individual rappers that made up the group, who then went onto become superstars in their own right. The latter method was usually more successful as the groups were signed based on their collective chemistry as hit-makers, based on each member's individual talent, i.e. the bar was set higher from the start.

In this medium, many of today's rap icons made their names. In the case of N.W.A., it was Dr. Dre and Ice Cube; with the Ghetto Boys, it was Scarface and Willie D; with the Wu-Tang Clan, the world was introduced to Ol' Dirty Bastard, Method Man, Rza, Ghostface Killa, among others; in the case of Digital Underground, it was Shock G and of course, Tupac Shakur, rap's greatest legend historically. In the early 1990s, an alternate format was a rap superstar introduced through his own independent label, in the case of Dr. Dre with Death Row Records, and Jay Z with Roc-A-Fella Records, among others.

Regardless of the various evolutions or reinvents of the format for breaking new rap superstars, there were always B-rate members of the MC's entourage who inevitably came along for the ride. In many ways, the Junior Mafia was no different. Any of the afore-mentioned crews could only be taken as seriously as their mentor's involvement in the project, and with that reality in mind, Biggie threw himself into the project as executive producer and creative supervisor, which quite frankly, the album desperately required if it was going to become even a marginal success.

With the exception of Lil Kim and Lil Ceas, most of Biggie's crew could barely get through the bars in their verses, their voices were generic, their deliveries sloppy and unimpressive. What drove the Junior Mafia album were the choruses to the album's two hit singles, '*Get Money*' and '*Player's Anthem*', which Biggie, of course, rapped on himself, and which credibly became one of 1995's best selling singles and one of hip-hop radio's most popular anthems.

To a certain degree, Biggie's appearances on the album were self-serving in the interest of keeping his voice out there on the airwaves, in the clubs and coming out of the sub-woofers. Still, he was also clearly interested in putting his crew on as prominently as he could, "My little niggaz Junior Mafia is dope, and I got a lot of their people too, but that's on the down-low. The albums supposed to [be out] July fourth, hopefully. I'm working on some new shit, 'cause a lot of niggaz that I wanted to get with [but] couldn't at the time because of their schedules—are ready to do some different things, and I'm willing to work. 'Cause I figure the only way a nigga is gonna sell a lot of records is if he stays up in niggaz' faces."

The album was also a chance for Biggie to step out as an entrepreneur from Combs' shadow, but with his encouragement, as Smalls and partner Lance 'Un' Rivera released the album under their own label, Undeas Entertainment, distributed not through Bad Boy Entertainment or Arista Records, but rather through Big Beat/Atlantic Records. This in, and of itself, showed Biggie's seriousness, as he avoided going the route of a boutique-deal with Bad Boy, where he would have inevitably received more built-in support from Combs and Company. Still, Puffy did show up on the project, this time as a rapper himself on several versus, with Biggie acting as Combs' creative manager, as he explained "we're just trying to level it out.

When Puff sat me down and said yo, I want you to manage me; and before I said yes, I had to ask him why? He was like who could teach me how to be the best artist, but the best artist…It doesn't (adversely affect our relationship)…that's they thing. It's like when we sit there to make music it doesn't matter. I know what I want my music to do and he knows what he want his music to do. That's two positive minds together. All we trying to do is make hit records. " The bond between the two men had clearly grown, based both on professional success and personal friendship. The respect was mutual on many levels, one of them being Combs' willingness to avoid making money off Biggie's name by insisting the album be released through Bad Boy Entertainment, which he easily could have done from a legal standpoint. Instead, he clearly believed in Biggie's potential as an entrepreneur, just as Biggie believed in his as an artist.

Biggie worked hard on making the album, reflecting the general momentum of his life and career at that point following his own initial success with *Ready to Die*. Smalls was clearly looking to build an empire for himself as the *King of New York*. "These days (I'm) just waking up like nine o'clock in the morning, going to different record stores, catching planes, going to the studio, you know? Thinking of ideas for songs for myself and for Junior

M.A.F.I.A. Just workin'." To his delight, the group's debut album '*Conspiracy*' went gold…the standard at the time within the industry for such releases…and introduced the world to Lil Kim, the self-proclaimed 'Lieutenant' of the clique. A sexy look and delivery equally as sleek and sensual helped launch Biggie's protégé and lover, at the time, into her own mini-stratosphere. In 1996 her solo debut, '*Hardcore*', the second album released under Biggie's own label, Undeas Entertainment, became an even bigger hit than the Junior Mafia debut, selling platinum at retail And, it scored three hit singles at radio—"*Crush On You*," "*Queen Bitch*" and "*No Time*", the latter of which went to number one on the Billboard Rap Singles Chart.

Kim's appeal was naturally broader because of her image as an unapologetic hip-hop sexpot, also attributable to her natural skills as an MC. While Biggie ghostwrote much of her first album, Kim held her own as a star, and went on, in later years, to become one of hip-hop's most bankable female superstars. Combs also appeared on this project, and clearly enjoyed the freedom from his responsibilities as a CEO, focusing instead on developing his skill as an MC in his own right.

In general, despite the heat that had started coming his way from Tupac Shakur, as the infamous East Coast-West Coast beef was brewing, Biggie was enjoying his creative evolution as both an artist and entrepreneur. He seemed to derive particular pleasure from continuing to put Brooklyn on the hip-hop map, representing for his old stomping ground, and giving his childhood friends and peers a chance to make their own come up in the rap game, "If everybody ain't understand my shit is the bomb before it comes out, it ain't comin' out. Not just Lil' Cease, because them niggas know I get busy. If anything, I know the lyrics is on point. But it ain't just the lyrics. The beat's got to be on point. The beat has got to be some shit that Idaho niggas is lovin', Houston niggas is lovin', LA niggas is lovin'…everybody got to love that shit, dog.

It can't be no Brooklyn record. Fuck that, I love Brooklyn. That's my spot right there. That's where everything starts and ends, in B-town. But…niggas ain't buying' records. But I got love for my peeps though, because they represent." With Biggie's rising status as an entrepreneur and an icon for the East Coast rap revival, New York was definitely making its own comeback from the early 1990s dominance of West Coast rap. To that end, the success of the Junior Mafia would work to further cement Biggie's position as the East Coast's hottest MC, and the *King of New York*, and no longer merely the self-proclaimed ruler, but rather a trend-setter to follow.

"I mean I haven't figured out what (the East Coast-West Coast beef) was all about. I just know that it was something that was negative, that I would say fans ran with, the media ran with, a lot of artists ran with, and it's just something that got out of control. Also, as far as a divide and conquer situation, it would be self-defeating for me as a person having a record company, and a person that's trying to be successful all over the world, to alienate half of the country I'm making music for."

—Sean 'P. Diddy' Combs,
C.E.O. Bad Boy Entertainment

Chapter 9:
East Coast vs. West Coast

For Biggie Smalls and Co., it was just another night of recording at Quad Recording Studios in mid-town Manhattan on November 30, 1994, 1994. Smalls was working on the debut LP for his crew, the Junior Mafia, and his friend, fellow rap star Tupac Shakur was on his way over to contribute vocals to the album. In the game a few years longer than Biggie, Tupac had become something of a mentor to Wallace.

As Shakur recalled it, "Both Biggie and Puffy, they know I was the truest nigga involved with Biggie's success. I was the biggest help, the truest nigga. I didn't write his rhymes, but he know how much he borrowed from me. He know how I used to stop my shows and let him touch the shows, let him blow up and do his whole show in the middle of my show. How I used to buy him shit, and give him shit, and never ask for it back. How I used to share with him—my experiences in the game, and my lessons, and my rules—my knowledge on the game with him. He owe me more, he owe me more than to turn his head and act like he didn't know niggas was about to blow my fucking head off. He knew."

While Biggie was more laid back in person, Tupac was fast becoming a living legend and a media magnet following a series of high-profile arrests for charges ranging from a shoot-out with police in Atlanta, to an attack on film directors the Hughes Brothers with a baseball bat, to his more recent charge of sexual battery for an alleged assault on a groupie at a Manhattan hotel. Shakur embodied everything about the live fast-die young philosophy a hustler was supposed to. And, Smalls to a degree seemed to gravitate toward that raw energy, while managing to stay clear of the legal realm of Tupac's rebelliousness.

While Shakur had made his name as a West Coast rapper, he had spent the large part of 1994 recording an album (*Me Against the World*) and shooting a movie (*Bullet*) in New York. He had befriended Biggie, in the course of doing both. Smalls and Tupac appeared on stage together at several radio concerts, were photographed at clubs sharing drinks and socializing, as well as collaborating together on at least one recorded studio-track that would be released in the wake of both rappers' respective demise.

To say Tupac trusted Biggie would be an accurate statement, as it would to say that there were no reported signs of any outward conflict or beef between the two leading up to the night of the robbery-shooting of Tupac and his posse that would forever change their relationship, and that of hip-hop in a costal sense. More importantly, aside from some verbal competition between Bad Boy Entertainment and Death Row Records, in which Death Row was clearly the antagonist, there was no real conflict of any substance existing between the two labels, or Coasts they represented, prior to the aftermath of the attack on Tupac.

In fact, according to an interview with Rolling Stone magazine that Sean Combs did shortly after Biggie's initial success, P. Diddy credited Death Row with serving as a blue print of sorts for Combs as he built Bad Boy, and more significantly, that he and Suge were friends. "When we were in our beginning stages, Death Row was established. Bad Boy was kinda modeled after Death Row because Death Row had become a movement. We wanted to model ourselves behind the record companies that were movements, like

Motown, Def Jam, Death Row...Whenever Suge would come to town, he would come by the office. Whenever I was in town, he would come pick me up and we'd hang out...It was all cool. No way in the world I could foresee any problems."

In an interview with Kevin Powell for Vibe Magazine, Shakur described the events as they unfolded, from the Rikers Island prison hospital following the shooting. He included his recounting of the shooting, its impact on him physically and mentally, as well as his logic for blaming who he did in its aftermath. "The night of the shooting? Ron G. is a DJ out here in New York. He's, like, 'Pac, I want you to come to my house and lay this rap down for my tapes.' I said, 'All right, I'll come for free.' So I went to his house...Me, Stretch (from Naughty by Nature), and a couple other homeboys. After I laid the song, I got a page from this guy Booker, telling me he wanted me to rap on Little Shawn's record. Now, this guy I was going to charge, because I could see that they was just using me, so I said, 'All right, you give me seven G's and I'll do the song.' He said, 'I've got the money. Come.' I stopped off to get some weed, and he paged me again. 'Where you at? Why you ain't coming?' I'm, like, 'I'm coming, man, hold on.'

I met him through some rough characters I knew. He was trying to get legitimate and all that, so I thought I was doing him a favor. But when I called him back for directions, he was, like, 'I don't have the money.' I said, 'If you don't have the money, I'm not coming.' He hung up the phone, then called me back: 'I'm going to call (Uptown Entertainment CEO) Andre Harrell and make sure you get the money, but I'm going to give you the money out of my pocket.' So I said, 'All right, I'm on my way.' As we're walking up to the (Quad Studios), somebody screamed from up the top of the studio. It was Little Caesar, Biggie's (the Notorious B.I.G.) sideman. That's my homeboy. As soon as I saw him, all my concerns about the situation were relaxed.

"I was with my homeboy Stretch, his man Fred, and my sister's boyfriend, Zayd. Not my bodyguard; I don't have a bodyguard. We get to the studio, and there's a dude outside in army fatigues with his hat low on his face. When we walked to the door, he didn't look up. I've never seen a black man not acknowledge me one way or the other, either with jealousy or respect. But this guy just looked to see who I was and turned his face down. It didn't click because I had just finished smoking chronic. I'm not thinking something will happen to me in the lobby. While we're waiting to get buzzed in, I saw a dude sitting at a table reading a newspaper. He didn't look up either. Black men in their thirties. So first I'm, like, These dudes must be security for Biggie, because I could tell they were from Brooklyn from their army fatigues. But then I said, Wait a minute. Even Biggie's homeboys love me, why don't they look up? I pressed the elevator button, turned around, and that's when the dudes came out with the guns—two identical 9 mms. "Don't nobody move. Everybody on the floor. You know what time it is. Run your shit." I was, like, What should I do? I'm think-ing Stretch is going to fight; he was towering over those niggas.

From what I know about the criminal element, if niggas come to rob you, they always hit the big nigga first. But they didn't touch Stretch; they came straight to me. Everybody dropped to the floor like potatoes, but I just froze up. It wasn't like I was being brave or nothing; I just could not get on the floor. They started grabbing at me to see if I was strapped. They said, "Take off your jewels," and I wouldn't take them off. The light-skinned dude, the one that was standing outside, was on me. Stretch was on the floor, and the dude with the newspaper was holding the gun on him. He was tell-ing the light-skin dude, "Shoot that motherfucker! Fuck it!" Then I got scared, because the dude had the gun to my stomach. All I could think about was piss bags and shit bags. I drew my arm around him to move the gun to my side. He shot and the gun twisted and that's when I got hit the first time. I felt it in my leg; I didn't know I got shot in my balls. I dropped to the floor. Everything in my mind said, Pac, pretend you're dead.

"It didn't matter. They started kicking me, hitting me. I never said, "Don't shoot!" I was quiet as hell. They were snatching my shit off me while I was laying on the floor. I had my eyes closed, but I was shaking, because the situation had me shaking. And then I felt something on the back of my head, something real strong. I thought they stomped me or pistol-whipped me and they were stomping my head against the concrete. I saw white, just white. I didn't hear nothing, I didn't feel nothing, and I said, I'm unconscious. But I was conscious. And then I felt it again, and I could hear things now and I could see things and they were bringing me back to consciousness. Then they did it again, and I couldn't hear nothing. And I couldn't see nothing; it was just all white. And then they hit me again, and I could hear things and I could see things and I knew I was conscious again.

But they knew me, or else they would never check for my gun. It was like they were mad at me. I felt them kicking me and stomping me; they didn't hit nobody else. It was, like, "Ooh, motherfucker, ooh, aah"-they were kicking hard. So I'm going unconscious, and I'm not feeling no blood on my head or nothing. The only thing I felt was my stomach hurting real bad. My sister's boyfriend turned me over and said, "Yo, are you all right?" I was, like, "Yes, I'm hit, I'm hit." And Fred is saying he's hit, but that was the bullet that went through my leg. So I stood up and I went to the door and…the shit that fucked me up, as soon as I got to the door…I saw a police car sitting there. I was, like, "Uh-oh, the police are coming, and I didn't even go upstairs yet." So we jumped in the elevator and went upstairs. I'm limping and everything, but I don't feel nothing. It's numb. When we got upstairs, I looked around, and it scared the shit out of me.

"Andre Harrell was there, Puffy [Bad Boy Entertainment CEO Sean "Puffy" Combs] was there, Biggie…there was about 40 niggas there. All of them had jewels on. More jewels than me. I saw Booker, and he had this look on his face like he was surprised to see me. Why? I had just beeped the buzzer and said I was coming upstairs. Little Shawn burst out crying. I went, Why is Little Shawn crying, and I got shot? He was crying uncontrollably, like, 'Oh my God, Pac, you've got to sit down!' I was feeling weird, like, Why do they want to make me sit down? I didn't know I was shot in the head yet. I didn't feel nothing. I opened my pants, and I could see the gunpowder and the hole in my Karl Kani drawers. I didn't want to pull them down to see if my dick was still there. I just saw a hole and went, 'Oh shit. Roll me some weed.'

I called my girlfriend and I was, like, 'Yo, I just got shot. Call my mother and tell her.' Nobody approached me. I noticed that nobody would look at me. Andre Harrell wouldn't look at me. I had been going to dinner with him the last few days. He had invited me to the set of *New York Undercover*, telling me he was going to get me a job. Puffy was standing back too. I knew Puffy. He knew how much stuff I had done for Biggie before he came out."

Most of the democratized world knows the rest of the story—the media and Death Row Records made sure of that. The short version: Tupac Shakur was in jail with a $1.4 million dollar bail required for his release pending the outcome of his appeal; Death Row Records' C.E.O. Marion 'Suge' Knight saw an opportunity to recruit Shakur, now at the peak of his notoriety and popularity, to increase his label's record sales ten fold; Knight bailed Shakur out in exchange for the rapper's signing a 3-album deal with Death Row, the first of which, All Eyes on Me, was recorded in 3 short weeks, and released just 2 months after Shakur's release from prison in the fall of 1995, just a little over a year following the shooting.

While in prison, Shakur had publicly named Biggie, Combs, Bad Boy Entertainment and, as a result, the East Coast at large, as being the responsible party for setting him up, even though all music fans and the media had to support the allegation was Shakur's claim, which was good enough for the press, which also saw the brewing beef as an opportunity to sell magazines and papers galore. As a result, they ran with the story as Tupac told it, sold the conflict one with roots not just between Shakur and Smalls, but rather between the East and West Coast at large, and rappers took sides accordingly. Once the wheels got rolling, there was no stopping it, and corporate America jumped on the bandwagon to get their hands in the cake as well. Knight and his roster of artists began assailing the East Coast as the weaker of the two in terms of talent, skill, and most importantly, sales.

Toward that end professionally, and his own personally, Tupac attacked Biggie in the media in every medium he could—television interviews, magazine interviews, on his albums, at his lowest claiming both in print and in a song that he had slept with Biggie's now-estranged wife Faith Evans, a claim she emphatically denied.

Knight also went on the offensive, claiming that Combs had been responsible for the shooting of Suge's childhood best friend and bodyguard, Jake Robles, outside a hip-hop event in Atlanta, even though there had been no formal charges brought by authorities following a thorough investigation. Puffy appeared to be most frustrated by this individual incident, specifically Knight's inference that he had anything whatsoever to do with causing the shooting, "Here's what happened…I went to Atlanta with my son. At that time, there wasn't really no drama. I didn't even have bodyguards, so that's a lie that I did. I left the club, and I'm waiting for my limo, talking to girls. I don't see [Suge] go into the club; we don't make any contact or nothing like that. He gets into a beef in the club with some niggas. I knew the majority of people at the club, but I don't know who he got into the beef with, what it was over, or nothing like that. All I heard is that he took beef at the bar. I see people coming out. I see a lot of people that I know, I see him, and I see everybody yelling and screaming and shit.

I get out the limo and I go to him, like, 'What's up, you all right?' I'm trying to see if I can help. That's my muthafuckin' problem. I'm always trying to see if I can help somebody…Anyway, I get out facing him, and I'm, like, 'What's going on, what's the problem?' Then I hear shots ringing out, and we turn around and someone's standing right behind me. His man — God bless the dead — gets shot, and he's on the floor. My back was turned; I could've got shot, and he could've got shot. But right then he was, like, 'I think you had something to do with this.' I'm, like, 'What are you talking about? I was standing right here with you!'" Still, Combs' couldn't help but take a shot at the mighty Suge Knight in the process, " I really felt sorry for him, in the sense that if he felt that way, he was showing me his insecurity."

As 1995 raged on, so too did the controversy, and the album releases from the West side, and by artists with no direct investment or stake in the beef—a prime example being Ice Cube, WC and Mack-10's collaboration album Westside Connection, which criticized the East Coast on any and every possible level, from their backpacks to their baggy jeans to their rappers. 1996 was hip-hop's biggest selling year to date, with Shakur's record sales alone generating $80 million for Death Row Records, and their distributor, Interscope.

In the end, the beef wasn't about anything more than making money, period, despite the fact that it cost both Biggie and Tupac their lives, so possibly it could be argued a tie in terms of who came out ahead. There were no clear winners outside of Death Row Records and Bad Boy Entertainments' parent companies, Interscope and Arista, and perhaps for Knight and Combs in terms of their net personal earnings.

Regardless of who was truly at fault…likely thieves with no connection to Bad Boy. Tupac was enraged, perhaps blindly, and in needing a direction to harness his anger, he chose the East Coast as an easy target. His interviews were a mix of legitimate anger and platinum trash talking—his specialty, "I have no mercy in war, they didn't have no mercy in war—they tried to shoot my fucking balls off!... So when I was in jail just sittin' there. I was gonna quit rappin' but then Puffy and Biggie came out in Vibe Magazine and lied and twisted the facts. All I wanted to do was end everything and walk away from the shit. I wanted to get out the game. I'm trying to get out the game and they wanna dirty up my memory. They wanna dirty up everything I worked for. So instead of quittin' it made me wanna come back and be more relentless to destroy who used to be my comrades and homeboys."

As the months wore on following Shakur's release from prison in the fall of 1995, he continued to amplify his verbal assaults and accusations at Biggie & Co., in the process fleshing out his theory on why the beef had now become a Coastal one. For Shakur, in large part, it was about loyalty, and he painted Biggie as the most disloyal player-hater in the game, claiming that Biggie had gone as far as to bite his style, in addition to everything else he was alleging in the grander scheme, "When I was in jail, Suge was the only one who used to see me. Nigga used to fly a private plane, all the way to New York, and spend time with me. He got his lawyer to look into all my cases. Suge supported me, whatever I needed.

When I got out of jail, he had a private plane for me, a limo, five police officers for security. I said, 'I need a house for my moms', I got a house for my moms. I promised him, 'Suge, I'm gonna make Death Row the biggest label in the whole world. I'm gonna make it bigger than Snoop even made it.' Not stepping on Snoop's toes; he did a lot of work. Him, Dogg Pound, Nate Dogg, Dre, all of them-they made Death Row what it is today. I'm gonna take it to the next level...It's not like I got a beef with New York or nothing, but I do have problems. And I'm representing the West Side now.

There's people disrespecting the West Coast. 'It's only gangsta shit—it ain't creative enough, it's fucking up the art form'—even though we made more money for this art form than all those other motherfuckers. The artists now, who selling records stole our style. Listen to 'em. Biggie is a Brooklyn nigga's dream of being West Coast…Let's be real. Be real…doesn't Biggie sound like me? Is that my style coming out of his mouth? Just New York-tized. That big player shit. He's not no player—I'm the player."

Shakur was definitely the most focused in his attacks on the East Coast, namely because he had the most personal stake in the beef where there was one at all. The problem was, because he was also hip-hop's biggest star at the height of the conflict between Death Row Records and Bad Boy Entertainment, he used his star power to raise Biggie's profile as the biggest target on the Eastern side of the battle field, which inevitably worked to help Biggie in terms of popularity and loyalty locally in NYC. In this way, perhaps Biggie, remaining as silent as he did during the majority of Shakur's attack over the course of 1995, was a strategic move. It was one, in which he laid back and soaked up the inevitable media limelight that was being shown him, as they positioned him as Shakur's main rival, as well as the West Coast at large.

Still, there is very little to dispute that Tupac was the mastermind, the field general if you will, taking orders (or encouragement) from Suge up on high, prodding Biggie along as he attempted to pit the East Coast against Smalls. Shakur's problem was Biggie had too much love from New York for the city to ever pick Tupac over Smalls in a rivalry, which played itself out opposite from how Tupac had planned it, further cementing Biggie's backing on his home turf. Biggie also distinguished himself as the more diplomatic or adult of the two, in the sense that he appeared to be very much above the whole beef—at least publicly. Still, he had an opinion the whole time, which he worked to keep to himself, as he revealed later on in an interview, namely rooted in the fact that he felt he was the better man, and the better rapper for not responding.

Most importantly, that his silence made Shakur look that much the weaker of the two, "He got the streets riled up because he got a little song dissin me, but how would I look dissin him back? My niggas is, like, 'Fuck dat nigga, that nigga's so much on your dick, it don't even make no sense to say anything." Shakur, for his part, kept plugging ahead with his diss, attempting to paint himself as New York's most important advocate, even as he raged against it, "I worked hard all my life as far as this music business to bring about East Coast /West Coast love and make everybody feel comfortable. I dreamed of the day when I could go to New York and feel comfortable and they could come out here and be comfortable. So, when people ask me about this East Coast/West Coast thing, it's not silly at all."

Shakur continued, "I love the East Coast..I come from the East Coast, but they have to understand you just can't be saying shit about us and think we're not gonna take it personally...You just can't be calling us fakers and pretenders and non-creative and say we can't freestyle...As soon as the East Coast separates themselves from Biggie we will do shows in the East.. Everything is beautiful...but so far the East Coast has been with him. Everything I read...every letter I read...every interview I read ...niggas keep saying 'Fuck 2Pac..Biggie Biggie this and Biggie Biggie that, like he's representin' everyone from the East Coast. That's why I attack the way I do...When I got out of jail the East Coast / West Coast shit was really started.

California Love, when I was singin' put it down, and now niggas is mad because money is fucked up. Attitudes have changed...It's not as safe as it used to be...I wouldn't sit down and have a conversation with Puffy and Biggie...because that's like Scarface sitting down with the dude he's hoping to rule. They are not on my level...but I can sit down with the OGs and from there [back east] which we are doing. People need to now we're not beefing with the East Coast..

We're about to start Death Row East with Eric B and all the OG niggas out there. We got Big Daddy Kane....Christopher Williams...we're trying to get Bobby Brown. We're trying to get the

East coast Death Row to be like the West Coast Death Row and make it major. We're not doing that until we get this business settled. Even while we're doing this we're trying to get Wu-Tang. I feel as though they represent the East Coast the way we represent the West Coast and I love them. If everybody's raps is what they really think, then everybody should understand what I'm doing... Chino XL, Mobb Deep , Bad Boy, Biggie, Lil Ceasar, Junior Mafia all of them is on our hit list."

For Biggie and Combs' part, they kept a relatively low profile as a team, giving few interviews in which they directly addressed or elaborated on Shakur's allegations, either regarding the shooting or that Shakur had slept with Biggie's wife. At the 1995 Source Awards, following a verbal assault from Knight from the main stage podium, criticizing his creative involvement in his artists' records and videos, Combs' responded diplomatically, attempting to play down any controversy, and praising Knight and Co. for their successes. Hugging Snoop Dogg before handing him his award, he stated, "I would like to congratulate Death Row Records on their success. I'm proud of Suge Knight and Dr. Dre."

Privately, he was even more confused, "I couldn't believe what he said...I thought we was boys." Still, as much as Combs and Smalls' silence on the beef in the media could be viewed as an attempt to avoid inflating it, their very silence on the subject naturally worked to, something they had to be aware of to some degree. Combs' was the first to know that in the entertainment business, any press is good press, and from an alternate vantage point, it could be argued that the silence on Bad Boy's part was very much a deliberate calm before their own storm with Biggie's new LP pending release.

By the end of 1996, all during which Biggie was hard at work on the aforementioned follow-up album to Ready to Die, entitled Life After Death, Smalls had had enough, and was ready to speak out to some point on the beef. Still, even in doing so, he kept a very real profile, avoiding counter-allegations or attempts to slander

Shakur's character personally, or really professionally for that matter. Biggie was clearly attempting to be the better man of the two, and it came across as such to fans, "I'm still thinking this nigga's my man…This shit's just got to be talk, that's all I kept saying to myself. I can't believe he would think that I would shit on him like that."

Puffy also seemed to display credible confoundment at the source of the beef, and genuine pain at its growing prevalence in hip-hop, "I'm hurt a little bit spiritually by all the negativity, by this whole Death Row-Bad Boy shit…I'm hurt that out of all my accomplishments, it's like I'm always getting my most fame from negative drama. It's not like the young man that was in the industry for six years, won the ASCAP Songwriter of the Year, and every record he put out went at least gold.…All that gets overshadowed. How it got to this point, I really don't know. I'm still trying to figure it out."

To B.I.G., the two had always been boys. They had met first during Tupac's filming of Poetic Justice in 1993, and kicked it again on the set of the Junior Mafia's Party and *Bullshit* video set, and cliqued immediately, such that, to Biggie, "I always thought it to be like a Gemini thing…We just clicked off the top and were cool ever since…Honestly, I didn't have no problem with the nigga." Still, Biggie did go out of his way to dispute Tupac's claim that he (Shakur) had been Biggie's mentor on the ways of the player, "There's shit that muthafuckas don't know. I saw the situations and how shit was going, and I tried to school the nigga. I was there when he bought his first Rolex, but I wasn't in the position to be rolling like that. I think Tupac felt more comfortable with the dudes he was hanging with because they had just as much money as him."

As Biggie went onto tell it, it was in fact *he* who had shared his experiences in the game with Tupac, versus the other way around. From Smalls' point of view, "He can't front on me…As much as he may come off as some Biggie hater, he knows. He knows when all that shit was going down, I was schooling a nigga to certain things—me and [Live Squad rapper] Stretch—God bless the grave. But he chose to do the things he wanted to do. There wasn't nothing I could do, but it wasn't like he wasn't my fault."

Though time had passed from the time of the shooting, it seemed Biggie still hadn't completely processed the fact that Tupac hated him with such venom, since the two had been so close before. A prime example of this was at the beef's peak, Tupac allegedly pointed a gun at Biggie from a car window outside the Soul Train awards, such that "That was the first time I really looked into his face…I looked into his eyes and I was, like, Yo, this nigga is really buggin' the fuck out." Biggie denied the gun-waving incident, but acknowledged Tupac was definitely acting out the role of a wise guy, so much so that even he was impressed by it in terms of what he viewed as Tupac's theatrical talents in playing the part he was, "Pac didn't pull steel on me (but) he was on some tough shit, though. I can't knock them dudes for the way they go about their biz. They made everything seem so dramatic. I felt the darkness when he rolled up that night.

Duke came out the window fatigued out, screaming 'West Side! Outlaws!' I was, like, 'That's Bishop [Tupac's character in the movie Juice]!' Whatever he's doing right now, that's the role he's playing. He played that shit to a tee.'"

Combs, once he did decide to speak out alongside Biggie, also questioned the basic logic behind Tupac's claim that he would set him up, pointing out that the way it went down wasn't his style anyway, were he to be party to such an action, "Why would I set a nigga up to get shot?…if I'ma set a nigga up, which I would never do, I ain't gonna be in the country. I'ma be in Bolivia somewhere."

In elaborating on why neither he nor Biggie had any motive to want Tupac set up in such a potentially lethal way, Combs also went out of his way to emphasize the friendship between Smalls and Shakur, and to point out that both he and Biggie wanted to keep things on that level, even in terms of the future post-conflict,

"I mean he was hurt, not because of the words, but because he didn't really understand why this man had so much hatred for him, you know what I'm saying?

Biggie nor myself had nothing to do whatsoever of Tupac being robbed or shot in New York City at the studio…[We] had no, had no knowledge of him going to be robbed. And that's just a fact. Anything else is a fantasy. And when Biggie heard it, he was hurt by it, because he really regarded Tupac as a friend. They had good times, that's how they met. Their relationship before that situation is that they were friends, and he would never do nothing, nor myself or anybody associated with me, would have never done nothing to hurt him. And in fact, he had helped us when Biggie was first getting out there. They were together, he would let Biggie open dates for him and he was appreciative and I was appreciative.

And it was a shock to us and it's something that we tried our best to do anything to alleviate any type of negativity as far as that situation. That's why we never made any records going back, we never made any negative statements, and the statements that we did say were that we wanted a resolution to it in a positive way."

In Combs' eyes, the whole claim was ludicrous and rotten from its roots on up, to the point where he suggested Shakur might even be using Biggie and Combs as a scapegoat to avoid his having to confront the real shooters in the macho stance he so eagerly took with Bad Boy. Combs' on this level almost seemed to pity Tupac, viewing his entire predicament as sad, "He ain't mad at the niggas that shot him; he knows where they're at. He knows who shot him. If you ask him, he knows, and everybody in the street knows, and he's not stepping to them, because he knows that he's not gonna get away with that shit. To me, that's some real sucker shit. Be mad at everybody, man; don't be using niggas."

Clearly, Combs was advising Biggie on how to handle the situation, such that Smalls might have handled matters differently had Diddy not had his future in mind, "The whole reason I was being

cool from Day One was because of that nigga Puff. 'Cause Puff
don't get down like that." Still both men felt the matter had gotten
out of hand, and were looking to put an end to it once and for all,
one way or the other, as Combs explained, seeming resigned to the
fact that it at that point, it had gotten so big there was no avoiding
it, "I'm ready for it to come to a head, however it gotta go down,"
he says. "I'm ready for it to be out my life and be over with. I mean
that from the bottom of my heart. I just hope it can end quick and
in a positive way, because it's gotten out of hand."

In addressing the rumors that Death Row had taken a hit out on
Puffy's life over the Jake Robles murder, Combs attempted to walk
the fine line between outlining his desire to avoid a violent end to
the conflict without sounding soft in the same time. Diddy clearly
felt he was above the entire thing, not because he or Biggie were
better than anyone else as people, but rather as professionals as Bad
Boy tried to keep it all business, "I never knew of my life being in
danger...I'm not saying that I'm ignorant to the rumors. But if
you got a problem and somebody wants to get your ass, they don't
talk about it. What it's been right now is a lot of moviemaking and
a lot of entertainment drama. Bad boys move in silence.

If somebody wants to get your ass, you're gonna wake up in
heaven. There ain't no record gonna be made about it. It ain't
gonna be no interviews; it's gonna be straight-up 'Oh shit, where
am I? What are these wings on my back? Your name is Jesus
Christ?' When you're involved in some real shit, it's gonna be some
real shit. But ain't no man gonna make me act a way that I don't
want to act. Or make me be something I'm not." Historically,
Combs clearly had a vision he was pursuing, and felt that by playing the position he was, more defensive than Knight and Shakur's
clearly offensive one, laying the groundwork to be the last man
standing from a business stand point, "I ain't a gangster, so why
y'all gonna tell me to start acting like a gangster?

I'm trying to be an intelligent black man. I don't give a fuck if niggas think that's corny or not. If anybody comes and touches me, I'm going to defend myself. But I'ma be me-a young nigga who came up making music, trying to put niggas on, handle his business, and make some history." Combs and Smalls' ultimate game plan seemed to be to strike back on wax and on the charts, which they would certainly do, but not before a tragedy of epic proportions would end the life of Tupac Shakur, and therein serve as the catalyst for putting the East Coast/West Coast controversy to rest.

Tupac's death had a dramatic effect on hip-hop as a whole because he was the biggest star the genre had ever seen, and its first true living legend. There was no way around that, for Bad Boy, or anyone competing with him in the year leading up to his death. The only way Bad Boy could truly advance beyond Tupac was to have him out of the way. Still, this fact alone doesn't provide ample evidence to suggest that the camp was behind Shakur's murder.

One man who many suggested did see Biggie and Co. as responsible for the death was Death Row C.E.O. Suge Knight, who Shakur was riding with the night he was murdered. In fact, Knight was the only real eye-witness to the murder, and wasn't talking to police, or anyone else, about who he saw pull the trigger.

Soon thereafter, he was imprisoned on a parole violation, and thereafter kept his silence as the rest of the world pondered. The only comment Knight did make publicly regarding the identity of the shooter was to a Dateline reporter, in which he stated that if he had information about that individual's identity, he wouldn't reveal it to police, in spite of his friendship with Shakur, because he "didn't get paid to solve homicides."

Many in the media and law enforcement felt this was suspicious, and rumors began to circulate that it was in fact Suge himself who had set Shakur up in a hit, despite the fact that Knight was injured in the crossfire, a bullet grazing the back of his head, barely missing his spinal chord. Tupac had gone out exactly as he had prophesized on his own albums, and the hip-hop world, despite the immediate shock of the tragedy, was better prepared for it because Tupac himself had expected it.

As a result, his fans to some degree had become desensitized to the possibility, such that when it happened, the world was somewhat prepared. Most industry insiders also thought this would bring the East Coast-West Coast beef to an abrupt end, something that Biggie was clearly hoping for as he prepared for the release of his sophomore album, the double-LP aptly titled Life After Death.

"I'm just trying to make sense out of it…It's just so hard trying to make sense out of, you know, why he's not here."

—Sean P. Diddy Combs, C.E.O. Bad Boy Entertainment

Chapter 10
Life After Death

Following Tupac's death, Biggie, like the rest of the industry, was clearly ready for a new beginning. This spirit was clearly alive throughout the completion of *Life After Death*, as well as in Biggie's attitude, outlook, and answers in interviews leading up to the album's release. As Biggie painted it conceptually, very aware in the process of how he had grown personally as a person, and materially, as well as professionally as an artist. "Life After Death is like a new beginning...it's like I can talk about different things now; 'cause I can't talk about being on the streets broke anymore, 'cause I ain't broke no more. I can't rap about the hardship that I go through 'cause I don't go through no hardships no more."

Still, the hip-hop world was clamoring for details in terms of Biggie personally. They wanted to know about every topic, ranging from Tupac & the East Coast/West Coast beef to his relationships with Faith Evans and Lil Kim, to all facets of his personal life, to how he had evolved as a lyricist in the lapse between his first and second LPS. Biggie knew as much, and announced in an interview in the months before its release, in late 1996, that fans would indeed get just that. "Right now I'm to the point where my new album is done so all the questions gon' get answered. Everything that everybody was always wondering about all of the shit that

B.I.G. go through and B.I.G. never got in no magazine and said shit, he ain't never got on no record and said shit. He was just that quiet nigga, you know. I learned a while ago that real Bad Boys move in silence."

In maturing on all levels, Biggie had clearly sought to slow his roll as a wild child, grow up some as a person and artist, and handle his business at it grew, on all levels. To some degree, in opening up to fans in the media, Smalls displayed a desire to live that he had not had, just a short three years earlier in the course of his debut LP. Biggie was not ready to die anymore.

In fact, he spoke with a sense of both perspective and clarity in terms of not only his desire to grow in all areas of his life, but also what he needed to do in the process to advance that agenda, both personally and professionally. "It was basically a situation where it was a lot of fast living going on. I was young…20…21 years old…I was doing different shows for $30,000 apiece and you coming home with a million and a half in your pocket and you buy a house, you buy a car, and you moving fast. I was moving too fast, you know…the company that I was keeping, they was moving too fast.

Everything just came apart. You know what I'm sayin'? I had a streak of good luck…everything just came back around and I had my streak of bad luck…I wreck my car…I had problems with my wife…That whole East Coast /West Coast thing…Then, I got locked up. Now, when I was in the hospital for three months with a broken femur bone, it gave me a lot of time to sit down and contemplate: Is this how I want my life to go and, if it's not, what do I want to do to change it. So I started limiting my crew down to my immediate niggas. All the extra niggas got to go…all the extra. All the extra women gotta go. My peace of mind is more important.. my mom…my son…my daughter…my family are what matters to me now."

Biggie was definitely looking to avoid Tupac's fate as he ascended toward Shakur's popularity with his new album's release, and made the world readily aware of it. He was signaling to all that Shakur's death had had a profound affect on him and had clearly been an important part of what made him change up the pace of his lifestyle. "(Tupac's death) just kinda had me thinking that it could've happened to anybody. Tupac was at the peak of his career...His records were popular...He was making movies and just blowing up. Some of the things that he said on records about me kinda hurt me, but at the same time he was kinda stuck in the same mode that I was stuck in. He was a young nigga gettin' a whole bunch of money, he was drinkn' too much, smokin' too much, his entourage was too big. Here you got 40 niggas with you, and y'all all doin' one thing. It's kinda hard to be the one to say I don't wanna do that."

In discussing his reaction to the news of Tupac's death for the first time publicly, Biggie expressed a deep sense of sorrow for the way things had resolved themselves so violently in the context of the beef as it was blown up on a national level. Still, it was clear he had reconciled within himself any question concerning his own responsibility for causing Tupac's fate, in that he had remained diplomatic throughout Shakur's attacks and the controversy that ensued. This was part of Bad Boy's strategy from day one, in terms of not getting too caught up in the media whirlwind surrounding and propelling the beef toward its tragic conclusion.

Most revealing in Biggie's explanation of how the murder affected him, was the fact that he had been sobered by it, as had everyone else throughout the industry at large. "When I heard about it, I think me and Little Cease' was at a restaurant in New York. Somebody paged me and told me about it. I was hearing that he was dead everyday that week...you know how rumors are. So, everyday I was hearing different things. But everything I was hearing I wasn't paying too much attention to...I knew Tupac. It wasn't a situation where he was just another person in the industry who got shot. We shared a lot of shit together so I know how strong he is. When he got shot, I was more or less like okay, he got shot. He's gonna recover from this like the last time, get up and make a record about it. Then when I heard that he really was dead, I was like awe shit, this is real."

On another level entirely, Biggie continued to play the diplomatic role in terms of acknowledging Tupac's talent and legacy as one of hip-hop's greatest MCs, and its first legitimate icon. In doing so, he seemed to be attempting to help the hip-hop nation put Tupac to rest, in part so he could take his position as the new ruler of rap's coveted throne...whether he meant to do so deliberately or not. "All my niggas I love, even if I got something I got to say to them. I gonna always sit them down and tell 'em, you can't do shit this way. This way is gonna lead to this. When it get to this, there's only one way it could end up...I don't like that...I mean the nigga's so talented.

Sometimes I would go see Tupac in a hotel and it be like 9 o'clock he'd been done gone in the bathroom to take a shit and come out with two songs. He just wrote with a radio right next to him and some books on the toilet. He was just very talented. And I really hate for some shit like that to flush. The nigga just got caught up and I feel for his family and friends, you know what I'm sayin'. That was a great loss to hip-hop."

He also displayed some anger or frustration on a personal level with the fact that the two MCs hadn't been able to make peace prior to Shakur's death, as well as lash out at the media in a subtle way for taking something that was irrefutably personal and making it larger in scope and affect than it was ever intended to be. "That was my man, ya know what I'm sayin'? It was just a misunderstanding that got blown up. And it kinda made me sit down and think about it and I'm like damn we must be two powerful mothafuckas because they made a personal beef between me and the muthafucka into a coastal beef...(It was) the media. Tupac never said all you West Coast niggas need to hate the East Coast and I never said that all you East Coast niggas need to hate the West Coast. They just took it (like) He's from the West and I'm from the East....[it's] East Vs West."

Still, despite his personal grief and regret, Biggie still continued to emphatically deny any role in the shooting, questioning the basic premise for Shakur's argument as being equally ludicrous in Tupac's passing as it was the first time he heard it. "Tupac know who shot him. Listen to the song on his *Makavelli* album. He explains everything that happens that night. The niggas he talks about on that record are the Niggas he thinks had something to do with it. He knows. It was a situation where he couldn't make no money rappin' about the niggas who really shot him. Ya know what I'm saying. He needed that edge. I was that edge he was looking for. I feel like this, it was something tragic. I wish that we could have sat down and spoke about it."

More importantly, despite Smalls' desire throughout the conflict to sit down and make peace, even he acknowledged that, based on where Tupac was, personally and professionally, at the time leading up to his murder, and in that sense, that perhaps his fate as such was unavoidable. "You know actually, after Tupac had got shot in that studio, I only got to see him one time. And that was at Soul Train. And like I said before…the entourage, the moving fast, that was what he was into…that was what was on his mind. It was a real sticky situation, where guns had to be drawn…and you can't talk under those circumstances."

That had been Tupac's time, this was Biggie's time, and off the subject of Shakur. Smalls had an entire other agenda of topics to delve into—both on record and in interviews—ranging from the affects on him personally as a result of envy within the industry, to changes he would like to see on a wider scale within hip-hop. He wanted to remove some of the inherent negativity that often dictated trends in terms of atmosphere, attitude and relationships, in terms of loyalty.

Biggie had a larger vision for hip-hop, one that transcended Coasts and a plethora of other barriers, and stood for larger causes than petty rivalries and jealousies. There were social causes that needed to be addressed, and that Biggie was trying to turn the spotlight on. "The things I talk about on this album are things that have happened since I've been in the game, that I'm not really happy with. It's like I was looking at the whole situation of being a Black boy from Brooklyn and like the only thing he's done is rob, steal and sold drugs all his life. Dropped outta high school…on the road to nothing.

Ya know what I'm saying. Met the right people, got a record deal and blew the fuck up. Damn, I'm proud of him, [but when that happened] I didn't get that feeling from everybody. I got was a lot of hatred. I gotta lotta playa-hatin' muthafuckas that looked at me like aw, he ain't alla that. He thinks he's this…that shit ain't alla that. Fuck dat nigga!..Don't get me wrong. Two million muth-fuckas proved to me that they did love me. But at the same time you still have your nigga that gonna want to go for the throat, inside and outside the industry. You got your niggas on the outside sayin' yeah, he got on a Rolex watch, I'm gon' rob dat nigga. Then you got your niggas on the inside saying oh, he rapping about this and he rappin' bout that, I'm gone dis dat nigga."

As a result, while he felt the industry at large had a long way to go in that pursuit, he had been hard at work on it personally, "You're gonna have to grow, you can't be that one hard-core rapper makin' a buncha money, talkin' a buncha shit, smokin' a buncha weed, gainin' a bunch of weight…just being unhealthy with yourself. The thing is you gotta take control of your life, take control of your own destiny, look out for your family. That's what I'm trying to do."

In context of Biggie's discussion on the attempts he was making to get his personal life straight, he also elaborated for fans on the state of his relationship with estranged wife Faith Evans following his widely publicized affair with Lil Kim, "(Me and Faith aren't back together) but we got a relationship, you know what I'm sayin'? It's not a relationship where she hates me and I hate her like it was before…I always tell Faith that it feels like we've been married three times. I know I love her. I definitely love her…It's more than just a marriage now; we have a family."

On the subject of his children, Biggie was also working hard to be a full-time father to his kids as they got older, explaining in one interview that his intention was to be as much an influence as possible on his children as they got older, in large part to keep them out of trouble, and on the right path, "Its hard but I try my best. I grew up an only child. My mother went to school in the morning to work in the evening and to school at night. So me just being able to run around, it leads into a lot of things. I never had a father figure. And my mother being from Jamaica, she wasn't hip to the street…She couldn't really tell why she didn't want me in the street. She just knew she didn't want me in the streets. And it left my curiosity open. So, I'm definitely tryin to be a father and let my kids know why they should be doin things. Even though their mother will tell 'em, hearin it from a father will tighten it up a little bit."

Biggie also let fans into his living room in discussing his evolved musical influences, which bore directly on what direction they could also expect from his new album, but also on what his days were like in context of his success—what he enjoyed doing to relax, how he spent his evenings, who he spent them with, and so forth, "In terms of influences, I really didn't have any one particular influence. I loved everybody and I listened to everybody. I was the one who listened to everybody because that was the only way you're going to determine who's whack and who's dope…You see the Best of the Isley Brothers, the Best of the Stylistics, the Best of Al Green, Erykah Badu, 112 would be up in there too…, I like slow music. My life is so heavy that when I move around in the studio or go into the office and check on Lil Kim or the Jr. Mafia project or go over to Bad Boy, rap is all I hear. When I come home I don't wanna hear no hard-core shit. I don't want to hear nothing that's talking about killing. I just want to take off my clothes, jump into a Jacuzzi, light a few candles and relax."

Biggie's broadening musical influences reflected themselves in the variety of guests on his new album. As he explained," On my first album I only did one song with somebody else, that was the *Method Man* track. But on this new album I gotta lot of guest appearances with R. Kelly, Bone Thugs N Harmony, Too Short, Jay-Z, Angela Winbush, 112. Puffy got a new team of producers called the Hitmen. They came and did a lot of tight work. I got to work with RZA from Wu Tang, Kay Gee from Naughty By Nature, Clark Kent, Easy Mo Bee, DJ Premier and Havoc from Mob Deep. We got some tight beats."

As an overall person, Biggie had definitely grown during the three years between his debut success and his follow-up as the world anticipated the release of *Life After Death*. As Biggie told it in one interview shortly before his death and the release of his second LP, "It was a lot more comfortable (this time around). I wasn't broke! It was a lot more comfortable...I mean everything's a lot more smoother. It's just calm. In the beginning, I had the typical attitude of a young rapper makin money. Ya know, I was the partyin guy. I was the guy wit the girls, all the extra that came wit the game.

You can't live that kind of lifestyle forever. I learn from the other people's mistakes. I know when to say no. You learn to make the right decisions and pick the right choices." Combs recalled following Smalls' death in an interview with Kurt Loder on the latter, reflecting that, "As a person Biggie definitely, changed a lot...like there was on '*Ready To Die*'...it was real personal. He wasn't really enjoying making the music as much; he was just trying to give you his story. On '*Life After Death*' he really enjoyed making the music. And then he's had a son since then, and a daughter, and I mean, just his family life...he enjoyed his kids a lot more. And just as a person, he was growing as a person."

Wallace and Combs had become as close as brothers by this time, and their affinity and confidence in one another was touching to anyone watching or listening. And their relationship reflected itself clearly in their professional successes. They were a team, and as Biggie elaborated on, in one interview shortly before the release of *Life After Death*, Combs' tireless energy and pursuit of success inspired Biggie's complete trust and had earned his total respect. "The thing about Puff…sleep. (He) never sleeps. Always keep doing what you gotta do. Flood the market. If it's hot make everybody know it's hot…He sat me down and asked me 'Do you wanna be a gold artist that's strugglin?' or 'Do you wanna be a multi-platinum artist that's livin' good and takin care of his family?' He taught me the game. That you can please your people/partners and at the same time please other people all over. At the same time, he do call a lot of the shots. I mean he's the boss; you gotta listen to what your boss tells you to do. But I just try and have as much input in the work as I possibly can. I mean I can't tell Puffy (with his successful track record) how to do what he's doing. It just so happens most of my ideas he likes. So everything blends into our vision."

Biggie and Puff clearly had a direction and goal for the sophomore project, complete and total domination commercially and artistically, which Smalls elaborated on somewhat as it related to the psychology behind their creative and marketing strategy for the record, "You gotta put 100% into everything you do. I sit back and see so many other people with their sophomore projects and they be kinda…well ya know…a little bit shaky!…I don't wanna be part of that shaky crew. I wanna be a part of that Boyz II Men, TLC type—come out with their second albums that blow up to a magnitude that no one expects. I wanna take two million and make it look like six million (on *Life After Death*)!"

Biggie knew what was coming to him, and had been busy preparing—in his personal life, in the studio, and in terms of his growing with the times—branching out into non-musical ventures within and outside of the industry to maximize his growth potential, as he continued to ascend in hip-hop dominance. "I'm kinda like what they would call a hot commodity, right now. I got my own clothing line; I got my own label; I just started my management company. I already sat myself down and said I didn't want to be the thirty-year-old rapper waitin for an advance on the record deal. So I'm gonna take my money and do something with it. Have something to fall back on.

If the acting and the movies…if all that comes into play…if it's something I think I can handle. Right now we're workin on the Big Poppa's Chicken and Waffle Shop that set to open in NY at the end of the summer. Also trying to get in conjunction with Heavy D and start up this Big and Heavy Big Men's Store. Cause I mean there's big guys with money too. Why neglect us? And Puff's restaurant Justin's, I'm tryin to be a partner in that. I'm tryin to get a strip joint in Atlanta…Tryin to get life together. That was one of my mistakes early on in my career, just movin so fast…goin to fast. …and sometimes that speedin will lead to a hard crash. You gotta know when to press the brakes…I'm pressin the brakes…just relaxin. Get in the crib, watch some movies, hang out with my man Jay-Z. Things everybody else do. I can't really run up in the malls like I used to."

So I try to say
Goodbye my friend
I'd like to leave you with something warm
But never have I been a blue calm sea
I have always been a storm

—Stevie Nicks, Storms

Chapter 11
March 10, 1997

While everyone had their eyes on March 15, 1997, the release date for Biggie's new LP, *Life After Death*, no one saw March 10, 1997 coming. It would knock the wind out of hip-hop's lungs, and stop one of rap's most beloved MC from breathing, ever again. Most hip-hop fans agree that when Tupac died, he was at the peak of his career, he had released 6 albums, starred in 6 films, sold 15 million records worldwide, and in the last 8 months of his life, had cataloged over 130 unreleased songs that would set his influence as hip-hop's foremost icon to continue for years after his passing. In other words, to a certain extent he saw the end in sight, and expected he might not last, and had planned for it.

Just the opposite was true when Biggie met the same fate. Though he had just completed work on his sophomore double-LP following up *Ready to Die*, it had taken him 2 years to record, and his total catalog as a solo artist of released material at the time of his demise was 2 finished solo Lps and one group album by the Junior Mafia. Though Shakur had been in the game two years before Biggie came on the scene in 1993, Tupac had a work ethic that has gone unmatched to date in hip-hop, with the possible exception of Jay Z in terms of material output. He also had an incentive that Biggie did not, in that Tupac genuinely believed his time was short. Wallace, conversely, was planning ahead for the future, and as such, was operating creatively on an entirely different wavelength, wherein he took his time because he felt he could. This makes the circumstances surrounding his murder that much more tragic in the fact that no one was expecting what befell the world on March 10, 1997, least of all Biggie.

One could surmise the latter, from his location alone, at the time of the murder. He was in Los Angeles, a city he would have never dared to visit, just a year earlier, in as open and advertised (and therein vulnerable) a manner as he was that week. Biggie had spent the week wrapping production on the video for '*Hypnotized*', his first single from *Life After Death*, doing radio interviews, and on the night of his murder, attending a *Vibe*-sponsored industry party with a who's who of hip-hop personalities from both Coasts.

From all outward appearances, the event in part, was a celebration of the end of the East Coast /West Coast beef, that had dominated the previous year and a half, and a chance for Biggie to subtly flex his position as hip-hop's new Don. Sean Combs' confirmed Biggie's intent, explaining to Kurt Loder in an interview following the murder that "Biggie and myself, we decided to go out to L.A. because we shot the video (for *Hypnotized*) out there. It was just better production value out of Los Angeles, the place where they make movies and everything. So, we decided to go out there and shoot the video. And while he was out there he wanted to also do as much damage control as he could do as far as what was done to himself and his career as far as his so-called being involved in this East Coast/West Coast rivalry...So he wanted to go out there and make sure that the fans heard him say it. So he was doing radio interviews and press interviews, and also he was doing rehearsal for Spring Break and shooting his video, and that's all he was doing... (And at the *Vibe* party), we basically sat at a table all night and a lot of people were coming and giving us positive greetings. Everybody at the party was just having a good time and dancing. And we were sitting there just talking all night and just listening to everybody else's music, and listening to our own records and feeling a sense of proudness hearing our record and just seeing all the people dance to our music, 'cause that's why we got into this.'"

In an MTV News report that traced the rapper's steps throughout the night leading up to his murder, it was clear that no one expected what was coming:

> "**8 p.m.**—The night began at the Peterson Automotive Museum on Wilshire Blvd. in Los Angeles at a party hosted by "*Vibe*" magazine, Qwest Records, and Tangueray Gin to celebrate Friday night's 11th annual *Soul Train Music Awards*...The guest list was a who's who of the East Coast hip-hop world, including Busta Rhymes, Heavy D, Da Brat, Yo-Yo, producer Jermaine Dupree and, of course, Biggie Smalls and the head of his label—Bad Boy Entertainment—Sean 'Puffy' Combs...
>
> **9:30 p.m.**—According to sources we spoke to, the party really got going around 9:30 or 10:00 p.m., and Biggie appeared to be having a great time taking a table near the dance floor and chatting with friends. Indeed, one witness told us, there was no discernable concern about being in Los Angeles on the part of anyone in the Bad Boy group despite the fact that in the past, other East Coast rappers have been worried about traveling West...
>
> **12:35 a.m.**—The only apparent problem with the party is that it became overcrowded, and as is often the case in such situations in L.A., the fire marshals were called in and the party was shut down at approximately 12:35 a.m...
>
> **12:45 a.m.**—As you can imagine with the party suddenly closed, a lot of people poured out into the street and were waiting for their valet parked cars. The stories do become a bit sketchy here, but according to a witness who spoke to '*USA Today*', Biggie and Puffy came out

around 12:45 and talked to their friends about going on to another party…Puffy first had his car brought around. He drove off, and then Biggie and two friends (reportedly Lil Caesar from Jr. MAFIA and Biggie's bodyguard, Damian) got into his GMC Suburban and drove up to the light with Biggie in the passenger side…As best we can determine, Biggie's car came to a stop at a red light at Wilshire and Fairfax when another car (a dark colored Chevy Impala driven by a man described as African American and dressed in a suit and bow-tie), drove around on the right side. Six to ten shots were then fired from the other vehicle into the passenger side of Biggie's car. Panic obviously ensued and the Suburban drove straight to nearby Cedars-Sinai Medical Center, which in good traffic is no more than a five minute drive."

At 1:15 AM on March 11, Christopher Wallace was pronounced dead by emergency room doctors. Perhaps the most affected by the tragedy, in an immediate sense were Biggie's closest friends and label-mates, who had attended the party with him and been with him in the shooting's aftermath. Among those closest to both the rapper and the tragedy was Sean Combs, who, like rival mogul Suge Knight, had been among the only eye witnesses to the shooting, and to the last moments of Wallace's life.

As Diddy described both the shooting and its aftermath from his vantage point to Kurt Loder in an interview shortly after the murder, "So we stood outside for like five minutes, and we just talked for a little bit, just about regular things that we talked about. Just, he talked about his album a little bit, and just talked to me, we were just talking about things that two guys talk about…you know what I'm sayin, about the party, girls, whatever. And then we got into the cars. We just said that it's time to leave. My car was in front, Biggie was in the middle and then another security vehicle, which had the off-duty officers in it, was behind. And, we left out of the driveway of the parking lot, we made a right and as we made the right we were just driving and the vehicles were one behind each other, and I was looking straight ahead basically. And I just heard shots ring out, and when the shots rang out I had immediately—did the human reaction—I had just ducked down, and everybody in the car ducked down. And then our car still sped off, and I heard somebody say Biggie's car had got shot at, and so while my car was moving, I just opened the door and the driver… he stopped…and I had jumped out and I had ran to the car. And I immediately did that because I knew his leg was broke, so I know there's no way he could have made it out of the car…So when I went there to the car, and I opened up the door and he was (exhales)…opened up the door…and he was hunched over and I was trying to talk to him and trying to move him over. And I was trying to tell someone to call 911 but I just told…by the time they get out here. I didn't know what was going on because he wasn't talking back to me. .. So I just told one of the drivers in security to just jump in a car and take me to the nearest hospital…please. And we were rushing to the hospital and there were other cars that were with us, and other people that were just following us; and as we got there everybody helped him out of the car. And as we were driving I was talking to him but I wasn't hearing anything. He wasn't saying anything. And, and I was just getting scared because I was just like, I didn't know like, why isn't he talking to me? And I was just getting scared. So I just started praying over him and praying and just trying to tell him to stay in there…And then when we got to the hospital everybody had jumped out of the cars and helped to pick him up and got him on the stretcher and the surgeons, they had immediately rushed him back into the emergency room. And then I just…everybody there just dropped to their knees and started praying…cause it just didn't look good…it didn't feel good. And that's what happened. And then they came and told us that he had passed, and it was just unbelievable."

News spread like wildfire throughout Los Angeles, and soon after, around the country. By the next morning, anyone with access to a newspaper, radio or television knew of the tragedy. However, the night before, people were still in the initial stages of processing the news and reality of Biggie's demise, and perhaps the most difficult part of that process still lay ahead—someone had to call Voletta Wallace, Biggie's mother, and break the news.

Biggie's former manager Mark Pitts recalled calling Voletta with Lil Ceas to tell her about her son's murder. "It was really hard man, because we knew how close he and his moms was. She was really strong though, right from the time we told her. She was crying, but she was worried about how we were doing at the same time."

As Combs' himself expressed in an interview with MTV's Kurt Loder following the murder, it was the strength of both Wallace's mother and wife that was helping to get even Diddy through the tragedy on a personal level, in a time when he was expected to be strong publicly and professionally. "Biggie's mom and Faith and the children have been extremely strong. They've been…matter of fact…they've been strong for me and helping to hold me up. His mother is just such a beautiful woman, you know what I'm saying, and she's from the church, and I'm just so happy that their relationship was good when, you know, before he passed. She's a very strong woman. Faith is very strong. And I'm gonna be there for them, just like he would be there for them, to make sure that they're all right."

On a national level, Biggie's death, as it sunk in, had a unique resonation, both in that it was so close in proximity time-wise to Tupac's, similar in circumstance, and that the victim had been the next in line in terms of popularity within the industry. Moreover, while the country had suffered similarly through Tupac's death, Biggie's was no easier because of that fact, as it might have been assumed on a psychological level with respect to desensitization.

If anything, Biggie's murder was that much more painful, both because of its senselessness, and because of Shakur's, in that hip-hop fans were counting in a sense on Biggie to fill the void on both a skill and superstar level.

Even Death Row Records quickly issued a statement which reflected their own internal stun over the reality and implications of the news. "Suge Knight and the entire Death Row Records family are shocked and saddened by the death of Mr. Christopher Wallace, a.k.a Notorious B.I.G. We would like to take this time to express our deepest condolences to the family and friends of B.I.G. Having just had the untimely death of one of our own, Tupac Shakur, by way of the same senseless violence, we do sympathize with those closest to Mr. Wallace. A gifted rapper, we are sure that Mr. Wallace's passing will effect many and it is certain that he will be missed throughout the music industry by his peers and fans." While many industry insiders viewed Knight's statement as both politically and publicity oriented, from his prison cell, as Suge would later admit in an interview, "I was saddened, because I know what his family was going through the way we did with Pac."

Nine days after the shooting, on March 19, Biggie's funeral procession was held, appropriately, in the streets of Brooklyn, where, as MTV News reported, "Fans and rap figures flocked to the Brooklyn neighborhood of Fort Greene on Tuesday to pay their last respects to late rapper Biggie Smalls. The body of the Notorious B.I.G. (clad in a white suit and wearing a white hat) lay in state at the Frank E. Campbell Funeral Home on Manhattan's upper east side. Mary J Blige, Queen Latifah, Lil Kim, members of Junior Mafia and a host of rap stars gathered to pay their last respects...Then Biggie's body traveled via hearse through the streets of Fort Greene (the rapper's old neighborhood) in a funeral procession designed to give fans a chance to say good-bye to the performer...Following the procession, the body of Biggie Smalls was reportedly cremated."

Life After Death was released on March 25, 1997, just 15 days after Biggie's tragic murder. Debuting at # 1 on the Billboard Hot 200

Album Chart, the album received rave reviews across the board, and scored the top 10 hit singles. Where *Rolling Stone* had called Biggie's debut LP the strongest for a new hip-hop artist since Ice Cube's *Amerikkka's Most Wanted*, they hailed Biggie for continuing "his God-given gift of excellent metaphors, and on this album he has many good tracks…The only bitter note of this 2x disc album was that it was Biggie's last studio album before his tragic death" awarding it the same 4-star rating they had his debut.

The album would go on to sell upward of 7 million copies, and is considered to date one of hip-hop's most successful albums, both critically and commercially. Biggie's family, friends and label mates worked hard thereafter to preserve and celebrate his music and memory, in the process securing his legacy, by releasing a series of musical tributes, including the tear-jerking remake of the Police's *Every Breath You Take*, retitled '*Missing You*'. The song appeared on Puffy's first solo album, '*Puff Daddy and the Family*', completed largely before Biggie's death, and featuring him on several tracks.

Missing You shot straight to number one, and all of its proceeds, as a single, were donated to a scholarship fund set up in the names of Biggie's children, raising over $3 million. His mother, Voletta Wallace, set up a foundation in her son's name—'The Christopher Wallace Foundation'—and set about trying to move on with her own life, and to help hip-hop fans move on collectively. One way in which she attempted to do so, as it related to the latter, was to honor one-time rival Tupac Shakur's mother, Afeni Shakur, through her son's charity foundation. The two women also appeared together at the 1999 MTV Music Awards, to a standing ovation from the audience, to present the award for Best Rap Video to Jay Z for '*Can I Get a What What*', who in the wake of Biggie and Tupac's respective deaths had begun his ascension to the top of rap's now vacant throne. It was, just as Biggie likely would have wanted, it given how close the two were personally. On a personal level, Voletta Wallace did her best to focus on carrying on her son's memory through her grandchildren and through going on living her life as Biggie would have wanted her to. "I work in my garden, I take care of grandkids. I have a foundation running…I have work to do (in the name of his memory)."

"My thoughts Big I just can't define
Wish I could turn back the hands of time
Us in the 6, shop for new clothes and kicks
You and me taking flicks
Makin hits, stages they receive you on
I still can't believe you're gone…
Reminisce some time, the night they took my friend
Try to black it out, but it plays again
When it's real, feelings hard to conceal
Can't imagine all the pain I feel
Give anything to hear half your breath
I know you still living your life, after death

Chorus: Every step I take, every move I make
Every single day, every time I pray
I'll be missing you
Thinkin of the days, when you went away
What a life to take, what a bond to break
I'll be missing you"

—Missing You, P. Diddy & the Family

Conclusion
Missing You

There are no easy answers in the mystery surrounding the murder of Biggie Smalls. Perhaps the most challenging part of it all to accept is the very reality that there are, in fact, no tangible answers into who shot Christopher Wallace, nor why he was so violently and senselessly taken from the world, his family, and his fans.

The L.A.P.D. has spent more than six years investigating the murder, exploring every possible angle into who might have been behind the murder. The suggestion or inference that, as high profile a murder investigation as Smalls' was to the department, that they would have ignored evidence had it implicated their own corrupt officers is both ludicrous and insulting to the intelligence of the citizens of our society at large.

Who would let their own police department get away with such an action? Would any remotely competent District Attorney or Mayor, both elected officials, allow such activity to go on under their noses knowing they would ultimately be held responsible for it on election day? After the Rodney King beating and Los Angeles riots, would the L.A.P.D. really want that kind of negative press again?

Suge Knight is not an angel, and most people agree that he played a large role in blowing the personal beef between Tupac Shakur and

Biggie Smalls into a national one in the interest of selling more records. Still, however that Coastal beef may have played a peripheral or circumstantial role in claiming either Tupac or Biggie's lives respectively; but, it doesn't make Knight personally responsible for either.

Focusing on Suge Knight distracts attention and resources, both within the media and law enforcement. It keeps them from working the case more elaborately because Knight is a convenient suspect; and in essence, works to allow the real perpetrators of Smalls' murder to continue to get away with it. This is a tough argument to accept given all the hype that has surrounded Knight over the past decade, especially in context of the East Coast/West Coast beef; but it is the most logical one if anyone were to really work through its components.

The L.A.P.D. has, and have moved onto looking into more viable alternatives. It is not the media's job to solve homicides, nor the public's—we pay police officers to take on that ugly task. They are the only professionals trained to do so, and if we attempt to rely on anyone other than those individuals or agencies we traditionally have entrusted with that responsibility, then the whole system breaks down. Vigilant journalism does not behoove anyone but the stockholders of the papers, which these trash journalists work for.

Men like Brian Bloomfield and Russell Poole have no one's interests in mind besides their own—not the public's, and certainly not Biggie or Tupac's. Russell Poole is a disgruntled cop who was fired for under-performing, according to the L.A.P.D. Brian Bloomfield speaks for himself through his trash documentaries. We do not celebrate or honor the memory of Christopher Wallace by buying either of these men's stories, nor their products. The public is hungry for answers, and in time may get them. But, they only hold up the process by indulging tabloid journalism that is purely speculative and based almost entirely on anonymous sources outside of Poole.

Reputable reporters like Pulitzer Prize winning Chuck Phillips of the Los Angeles Times should know better, and should have the basic common sense to understand that no gang member would break his internal vow of silence to go on record about Biggie hiring him to commit the murder of Tupac, let alone risk directly implicating himself in that murder. Nor would Phillips, despite the journalist's vow to protect sources at all costs, truly conceal the real identity of Shakur's killers if he knew their identities. The pressure would be too great, from law enforcement, as well as from his own paper in terms of their own concern over civil and criminal liabilities from withholding evidence relevant to an ongoing murder investigation. The jail time wouldn't be worth it to anybody, and what purpose would it serve in terms of putting either man's memory truly and rightly to rest, outside of *selling more papers!!!!!*

Biggie's mother, Voletta Wallace, echoed the latter sentiment in her own statement to MTV news following the release of the LA Times article implicating her son in Tupac's murder, and spoke of the larger impact that trash news stories like those in the LA Times and related publications can have on the general mood surrounding her son's murder, and most importantly, how such a climate helped to precipitate and cause the very murder itself, "For a second I felt that my son was just murdered (again)…How do I feel? I'm downright angry. I'm a mother, I'm a human being and [*L.A. Times* writer Chuck Philips] is gonna attack my son that's not here to come forward and defend himself?…I haven't really read the article…I have nothing to say. If he is going to say something nasty or accuse my son, I'll have nothing to do with it. I just didn't want to have any part. News like that gets innocent people murdered. News like that causes hatred. News like that causes a lot of resentment."

The bottom line seems to be that until the investigators come up with real answers into who murdered Christopher Wallace, the media should stop making them up at random as they go along.

That kind of reckless and irresponsible reporting, at a very minimum, only works to cause Biggie's family that much more pain. On a larger level, it does the same for his millions of listeners.

Most hip-hop fans will agree they were unprepared for news of Biggie Smalls murder. Where there had been less surprise at the news of Tupac's drive-by slaying a year earlier, the only thing the two rap icons had in common in terms of their respective murders were the killings themselves in the context of the larger East Coast /West Coast beef. Biggie's death came as a complete shock to everyone on a personal level, even his enemies. No one uttered any editorial mention of his having had it coming through an antagonistic public persona within the gangsta lifestyle as they had so prominently with Tupac's murder.

Sadly though, those same pundits were quick to lump Biggie into that group due to the style of his murder—that of a gangland, drive-by nature so prevalent in West Coast street wars. No one pointed out that the latter connection could have been purely coincidental to the fact that Biggie happened to be in Los Angeles at the time of his murder, rather than it having anything to do with affiliations on his part, personally, to that crowd. None were ever credibly established.

Still, the media frenzy was once again in full flush. Immediately, the media headlines began recklessly reading in the vein of 'Another rapper lives by the gun, dies by the gun', or 'Gangsta rapper's persona catches up with him.' Biggie was not affiliated with a gang, and for anyone in the media that might have stopped to take the time and do their research correctly, they would have found that New York's borough/project set-up, as far as 'gangs' went, was 180 degrees opposite to that of the Los Angeles structure. There were no Crips-Bloods rivalries on the East Coast the way there were in a dominant sense on the West Coast.

More importantly, despite media attempts to link Bad Boy Entertainment to the Crips, conveniently the opposite gang from that which Death Row Records C.E.O. Suge Knight claimed affiliation based on his boyhood roots in South Central Los Angeles, there in fact, weren't any to speak of—at least from Sean Combs' and company.

Combs, for his part, went on record shortly after the murder to dispute outright the assertion that his label had ever been affiliated with the Crips, professionally, or in any other fashion, telling MTV News that "We've never hired Crips, or any other gang faction, to do security for us. But the misconception is that because we're young and we're black...like we're not handling business like anybody else. We're trying our best to handle our business just like any other businessman that's out there in the world. And it would be extremely unintelligent to hire gangs to do security for you. We have never, never hired any gangs for security...It's not possible. I have a small boutique label, and I take responsibility for everything that comes from my label, and I know for a fact that this is something that has never happened. And I heard y'all report about an affidavit from the Compton police, but I'm just here to say that it's not the truth. No one, and I see everything I sign off on... everything that's done...and I know the security that we hired were bonded security men and also off-duty California police officers. Just like...That's the same route Madonna would take or anybody that's in entertainment to, you know, Sylvester Stallone would hire bonded security people. And that's what we did."

By establishing the alleged gang link, media speculators began to lay out scenarios in which, because of the gang-land style of Biggie's killing, he must have had some beef with the Bloods, and therein, that conflict must in some way have been an extension of Bad Boy's beef with Death Row Records and Suge Knight. From this leap out of reality and into further fiction, the media, and then investigators who had no other leads, then began to focus in on Suge Knight as the alleged mastermind behind the murder, theorizing that he had arranged the hit from his prison cell in retaliation for the murder of Tupac, which he purportedly blamed Biggie Smalls for.

As unfounded in fact and as irresponsibly as this theory was reported in the press, behind closed doors, the police were equally as confounded as everyone else was concerning why, on a personal level, anyone would have had reason to desire Smalls' killed… other than the potential notoriety that went along with such a trophy. No one contested the theory that the drive-by killing was gang-related, just that the motive was anything more than a symbolic victory for the West Coast. Aside from wild theories from a lone, rogue L.A.P.D. detective Russell Poole, who left the force disgraced after alleging publicly that corruption within the Los Angeles Police Department's Rampart Division had played a role in facilitating and/or covering up officer involvement in the shooting, it remained an unsolved homicide.

As a result of the lack of information coming in about possible motives and/or credible suspects for the murder, the silence worked in the same way against Biggie as it had during the height of the East Coast/West Coast beef, when he and Combs' stayed relatively quiet, to create gossip, rumor, and pure speculation that the media, fans, and Poole, took as fact. From his prison cell, Suge Knight was briefly named as a suspect according to the LAPD, who despite serving four search warrants, turned up nothing in the way of evidence that ever led to Knight's being formally charged, accompanied by the fact that the L.A.P.D. eventually ruled Knight out as a suspect in the slaying.

An MTV News brief in April 1999 summarized the events surrounding the brief suspicion: "Death Row Records executive Marion 'Suge' Knight has been named as a possible suspect in the slaying of rapper Notorious B.I.G., according to the Los Angeles Police Department…Though Knight was already behind bars serving out a nine-year sentence at the time, police suspect he might have played a role in the March 1997 drive-by shooting of

the 24-year-old rapper, whose real name is Christopher Wallace...
On Tuesday, detectives served search warrants to four locations
that are linked to Knight...According to Lt. Al Michelena, business records and a 1995 dark metallic-purple Chevrolet Impala
were seized at the Death Row offices in Beverly Hills. The auto-
mobile matches the description of the vehicle used in the shooting,
which took place outside of a *Vibe* magazine party held at the
Peterson Automotive Museum in Los Angeles."

Over two years would go by before another official news story
alleging Knight's role would surface, this time in June, 2001, from
Rolling Stone Magazine and writer Randall Sullivan. He (not surprisingly) based his story on disgruntled former L.A.P.D. Detective Russell Poole as his main source, and laid out his silly theory,
fully, as he had for anyone in the media who would listen. The
article, titled "The Murder of the Notorious B.I.G.", would later
become a book by the same journalist entitled "*LAbyrinth: A detective investigates the murders of Tupac Shakur and Notorious B.I.G.,
aka Biggie Smalls, the implication of Death Row Records' Suge Knight
and the Origins of the Los Angeles Police Department Rampart
Scandal.*"

In both, Poole and Sullivan's principle source, claiming that Knight
had blamed Smalls for setting up Tupac's murder, despite the fact
that the Las Vegas and L.A.P.D. had already unofficially named a
suspect, Crips' gang member Orlando Anderson as the shooter—
who was, not surprisingly assassinated, following the Shakur slaying by the Bloods in retaliation for his role. Moreover, Poole suggested that several L.A.P.D. officers, namely former officer David
A. Mack, now serving a 14-year prison term because of his role in a
bank robbery in November, 1997, and a mysterious mortgage
broker named Amir Muhammad, who the L.A.P.D. questioned
and eliminated as a suspect in the Smalls shooting—based on his
having a solid alibi for the night of the murder—had carried out
Knight's masterminded plot.

Isn't it fairly logical to assume, within the murky criminal world of bank robbery, murder and prison, that Mack, if he truly had any credible information he could offer up on Knight's role in planning the murder, would in exchange for cutting his own prison sentence? Surely, Suge Knight is a much higher profile prosecution for the L.A. District Attorney than David Mack? If Knight had the power to reach out from behind bars and have Biggie killed, would he really be careless enough to leave Mack alive to potentially finger him to authorities? If Suge were that powerful, he wouldn't have been in prison in the first place at the time of the shooting.

Not surprisingly, behind the smoke and mirrors, Knight was nothing more than an easy target to pin the blame on, and despite the fact that law enforcement had seen through that and eliminated Knight as well, the media, in the interest of selling papers and magazines, ran with it anyway. In this light, Knight was becoming quite the whipping boy for networks like VH1, who, through a series of Behind the Music specials, branded him as public enemy number one, calling him 'Gangster Suge Knight', and recounted, largely through interview segments with Russell Poole, how the all-powerful Knight—from his jail cell—orchestrated the hit.

Ironically, in May of 2000, just a little over a year after they had first reported Poole's wild theory via the L.A.P.D., parent network MTV would publish its own update on the case stating that the L.A.P.D. was still seeking a suspect in the unsolved homicide, largely because they no longer suspected Amir Muhammad as the shooter: "A Southern California mortgage broker once suspected by police of being the triggerman in the 1997 murder of Christopher Wallace is reportedly no longer under suspicion in that case. Police had once theorized that Amir Muhammad had been hired as the hitman by Biggie's rap rival, now-imprisoned Death Row Records head Marion 'Suge' Knight, in association with Muhammad's longtime friend David Mack, a former Los Angeles Police officer, who is currently serving time for bank robbery...However, Wednesday's Los Angeles Times quotes an L.A.P.D. detective as saying the department hasn't pursued the Muhammad theory in more than a year."

Despite the fact that the L.A.P.D. had formally exonerated Muhammad, and in essence Knight, from having played any role in the murder or its plotting, the media horde continued as Trash Documentary film maker Brian Broomfield came out with his 100% fictitious documentary 'Biggie & Tupac', in which, to no one's surprise, Russell Poole again popped up. He was, obviously, in love with his own voice, desperate for attention, craving the same spotlight as the stars whose murders he had investigated, trashing Knight's name over and over again and pointing the finger at him. It seemed more than anything that Poole was determined to make his case to the public, if he couldn't make it to his own superiors, or from a witness stand to a jury—not in the name of justice however, but rather toward the end of his own 15 minutes of fame.

Suge, like Biggie had over the course of Tupac's verbal onslaught of attacks, taken the higher path, turning down virtually all interview requests related to the topic, and by remaining silent, refusing to stoop to the level of people like Poole and Broomfield to even dignify the laughable allegations. It seemed, as time distanced itself from the tragedy, that rather than let Biggie's memory breathe on through posthumous album releases and fond memories on the part of loved ones in occasional interviews about his life and times, the media preferred to keep the controversy surrounding Smalls' death alive…smothering his memory with its stink. Rather than let the police department do its job, journalists carelessly invented stories and theories that had no basis in fact, and did more to trample Biggie's legacy than to celebrate it.

Perhaps the best example of the reckless nature of the media-reporting that surrounded the slayings of Tupac Shakur and Biggie Smalls, came in September 2002. It suggested that the latter rapper paid the Crips street gang $1 million to execute the murder of his former friend and purported rival. This was recklessly reported, despite the fact that Biggie, in every published interview surrounding the East Coast-West Coast beef, made overtures to Shakur regarding the two settling whatever the conflict was for Tupac. And, it was written, in the face of the fact that neither the L.A.P.D. nor the Las Vegas P.D. had EVER uttered even a breath of a hint that they in any way, shape, fashion or form suspected Christopher Wallace of playing any remote role in Shakur's murder.

In a surprisingly reckless and largely unfounded article published in the Los Angeles Times on September 6, 2002, reporter Chuck Phillips laid out his laughable claim, purporting that "According to people who were present, the Crips' envoy explained that the gang was prepared to kill Shakur, but expected to collect $1 million for its efforts. Wallace agreed, with one condition, a witness said. He pulled out a loaded .40-caliber Glock pistol and placed it on the table in front of him. He didn't just want Shakur dead. He also wanted the satisfaction of knowing the fatal bullet came from his gun." While Phillips claimed that "a handful of thugs and East Coast rap associates" were part of Biggie's entourage when he made the alleged deal with the conveniently un-named Crips, when asked by MTV if he could name any of the alleged witnesses, the journalist replied "Not that I'm willing to talk about…All I'm going to say is that I think I have very good sources on the story."

Biggie's estate, run by his mother Voletta Wallace, responded by filing a defamation suit against the LA Times and Phillips personally for besmirching her deceased son's memory and good name, as reported on MTV News, "I will find peace when myself and my lawyers deal with Chuck Philips and the *L.A. Times.*"

Smalls' widow Faith Evans, in an interview with MTV News, reported that "My immediate reaction when I saw the article was definitely shock …and anger…We feel that it's this type of irresponsible journalism and widespread untruths that lead to people losing their lives, sometimes. We don't want it to continue to happen. It's just not right. Sometimes there is some truth in things you read and things you see on TV. This is a case where it's just not true…I was living in Manhattan. I was about eight months pregnant with our son C.J. The night (Tupac was shot) I remember B.I.G. calling me and crying. I know for a fact he was in Jersey. He called me crying because he was in shock. I think it's fair to say he was probably afraid, given everything that was going on, at that time, and all the hype that was put on, this so-called beef that he didn't really have in his heart against anyone…I think it would be some element of fear that would kind of run through his mind… given the fact that his name was involved in a lot of the situations involving Tupac, before his murder. He was already getting threatening phone calls. I'm sure…for all he thought…he could be next. Which ironically, months later, he lost his life as well."

Lil Ceas bolstered Faith Evans' claim that Smalls was in New Jersey the night of the shooting, stating that he was sitting next to Biggie on a couch in his condo watching the very Bruce Seldon-Mike Tyson fight that Shakur, Knight, and company were attending prior to the shooting, "We watched that fight at home…Big was in the studio, earlier that day…did what he had to do in the studio…then went back home and we watched the fight. We wasn't nowhere near Vegas."

Biggie friend and former co-manager Wayne Barrow further disputed Phillips' story by claiming that he was with Smalls in New York the day of Shakur's murder preceding the fight, "I was actually with B.I.G.…B.I.G was in the [Daddy's House Recording] studio. 'Nasty Girls' is the record we was recording. Him being able to be in two places at one time…he must be a genie…(MTV reported that representatives for Voletta Wallace have produced documentation from Daddy's House purportedly confirming what Barrow recollected.).

In terms of where he was, during that day, that was the course of the day…It's impossible for him to make it in time for the fight. I

153

just can't see it—unless he chartered one of them type of jets to get you from New York to England in two hours. B.I.G didn't have that type of paper to be maneuvering like that."

Though the Los Angeles Times stood by its story, most of the public dismissed it as tabloid garbage. Still, its presence in the mainstream media, and the fact that historically credible news publications like the Los Angeles Times and even Rolling Stone Magazine would contribute to that presence, is perhaps most disturbing. It is the duty of the free press to report news…yes…but, with that freedom comes an equally as enormous obligation to do so responsibly. And, it should be done in a manner that avoids, at all costs, reckless reporting like that which has dominated the mystery surrounding the murder of Tupac Shakur, and especially Biggie Smalls.

The very fact that Wallace was murdered, at all, is in and of itself puzzling, given the kind of human being and professional he was within his own industry. What is more confounding to those of us who remember Biggie as such is to try and understand why the media, rather than besmirch his name and legacy to sell papers, wouldn't try to do so by celebrating it? Fans would react equally as enthusiastically at news stands, probably more so.

All we have left of the Notorious B.I.G. is his music and his memory, and it is everyone's responsibility, as humans, to do their best to preserve Wallace's legacy for the sake of his family, first and foremost, and for hip-hop at large. As we look back on Biggie Smalls years from now, we will rap along to his rhymes, dance along to the beats that lay beneath them, educate our children as listeners on his importance to hip-hop historically, and inevitably, have to consider his death in understanding his overall legacy.

Still, in doing so, don't we owe it to his memory, to all the good times and greatest hits he gave us over the course of his short career, to do so responsibly and accurately according to the facts in the record, and nothing else? To some degree, it is healthy as listeners to ponder why we're remembering or celebrating Christopher Wallace, at all? When we do, it becomes quickly clear that it is because of who he was in his life, not who the media has tried to make him in his death. Doing so will help keep the importance of preserving Biggie's memory with as much dignity as he left it to us with, in part by turning a deaf ear to those who seek to make his death the most memorable part of his lifetime. It should be the reverse. Take how Wallace conducted himself in the course of the East Coast /West Coast controversy as the best example of how he would want us to act as fans and people in respect of the dead. By doing so, we are left only with Biggie's life and times to reflect on, which is what he would have wanted in his life after death.

Discography:

Albums:

Ready To Die —Bad Boy/Arista 1994 Platinum X 3
Life After Death—Bad Boy/Arista 1997 Platinum X 10
Born Again—Bad Boy/Arista 1999 Platinum X 2

Singles:

Party and Bullsh*t
Juicy—Gold
Big Poppa—Platinum
Warning—platinum
One More Chance (Stay With Me)—Platinum
Hypnotize—Platinum
Mo Money Mo Problems—platinum
Sky's The Limit feat. 112
Nasty Boy—Remix feat. Lil' Kim
Loving You Tonight Ft. R. Kelly
Dead Wrong
N.o.t.o.r.i.o.u.s
Biggie/Would You Die For Me?

Guest Appearances:

Real Love w/Mary J. Blige
Bunch of N*ggas w/Heavy D
Dolly My Baby—Remix w/Supercat
What's The 411—Remix w/Mary J. Blige
How Many Ways—Rmx w/ Toni Braxton And Puff
Da B-Side w/Da Brat
Jam Session w/ Heavy D
Bust A Nut w/ Luke Campbell
Who's The Man w/ Dr.Dre & Eddie Lover
Flava In Ya Ear—Rmx w/Craig Mack, Rampage, L.L.Cool J & B.
Rhymes
For My N*ggaz w/Red Hot Lover Tone, Grand Puba, and M.O.P.
Let's Get It On w/Eddie F & The Untouchables, Grand Puba and
Heavy D Cunt Renaissance w/Crustified Dibbs
Young G's Perspective w/ Junior M.a.f.i.a. & Black Jack
Nine Dog MCs w/ Red Bandit, Grand Puba, Grandaddy I.U., and
others
Think Big w/Pudgee and others
This Time Around w/Michael Jackson
Can't U See w/Total
Player's Anthem w/Junior M.A.F.I.A.
Get Money w/Junior M.A.F.I.A.
(You To) Be Happy w/R. Kelly
Bust A Nut w/Luke
Get Money—Remix w/Junior M.A.F.I.A.
Brooklyn's Finest w/Jay-Z
Only You w/112
Young G's Perspective w/Blackjack
You Can't Stop The Reign w/Shaq
Drugs w/Lil' Kim
Crush On U w/Lil' Kim and Lil' Ceas
Keep Your Hand's High w/Tracey Lee
Stop the Gunfight w/ Trapp and Tupac

Victory w/Puffy feat. Busta Rhymes
House Of Pain w/ Stretch and Tupac
Victory—Remix w/Puffy feat. Busta Rhymes
Been Around The World w/Puffy feat. Mase
Young G's w/Puffy feat. Jay Z
It's All About The Benjamins—Remix w/Puffy feat. Lil' Kim & The Lox
Buddy X (remix) w/ Neneh Cherry
Live at the Palladium w/Funkmaster Flex feat. The Ol' Dirty Bastard
Stop the Break w/ DJ Ron G feat. KRS-ONE & others
The Points w/ Bone Thugs, Buckshot, Big Mike, Ill & Al Scratch etc.
Real Niggas w/ Puff Daddy & Lil' Kim
Why You Trying To Play Me w/ Aaron Hall

Compilations:

Hip-hop's Most Wanted—"One More Chance" (Remix)
The Box's Hip-hop Number One Hits—"Juicy"
The Ultimate Hip-hop Party 1998—"One More Chance/Stay With Me"
The Ultimate Hip-hop Party 1998—"Gettin' Money" (The Get Money Remix)
Panther Soundtrack—"The Points"
Funkmaster Flex Mix Tape—Volume 2 "Da Lox and Biggie Freestyle"
The Show Soundtrack—"Me And My B*tch" (Live)
Who's The Man? Soundtrack—"Party and Bullshit"
NBA Jam Session—"Jam Session"
MTV Party To Go—Volume 8
Funk Master Flex & Big Cap -The Tunnel—"MSG Live Freestlye"
Lyricist Lounge 2—"16 Bars"
Bahlers Forever—"Why You Trying To Play Me

ABOUT THE
Christopher Wallace Memorial Foundation

The Christopher Wallace Memorial Foundation *(CWMf)* was founded in October 1997 by Ms. Voletta Wallace after the death of her son, Christopher (aka Notorious B.I.G.). CWMf serves to provide scholarships and grants, books, leading-edge computer hardware/software and other fundamental learning tools to children. CWMf seeks to secure contributions, which will allow CWMf to fulfill its mission and achieve its goals.

MISSION: The Tools to Build Our Future

CWMf's mission is to provide the literacy tools—primarily books and computers—that our young people need to build and protect their future, be successful overall in their endeavors and become positive contributors within their communities.

EVENTS INCLUDE

A B.IG. NIGHT OUT New York City, NY

Every year the Christopher Wallace Memorial Foundation holds a black-tie dinner to raise funds for children's school equipment and supplies and to honor the memory of the Notorious B.I.G. (For the event, B.I.G., in addition to referencing Biggie's name, stands for Books Instead of Guns.

Charter Schools

Many of these newfound schools provide the alternative education and attentive instruction that "traditional" education systems may no longer provide to all students equally. CWMf would like to provide financial assistance to enroll "gifted" candidates into these highly conducive learning environments and make sure that the resources remain equally distributed among students.

Technology Centers
To draw much needed attention to existing technology support, instruction and access centers across the country, CWMf will work with celebrity/entertainment personalities to endorse its "Adopt-A-Tech Center" program.

Creative Arts Programs
Christopher Wallace was a creative genius and CWMF feels a natural affinity to help other talented young "art"-trepreners use books and computers to obtain knowledge and explore career opportunities early in their pursuits

FOUNDATION GOALS

CWMf possesses a renewed sense of commitment and focus to help nurture the minds of our youth. As part of their initiative, CWMf will identify deserving institutions and organizations, including:

THINK B.I.G. Community Center—Bedford Stuyvesant, NY
The foundation's ultimate goal is to build and establish a community center in the Brooklyn neighborhood in which Christopher was born and raised. The center will provide a day care center, after-school tutoring, technology lab and computer-training program and house the administrative arm of the foundation.

Early Childhood Development (Day Care) Centers
It is important that learning software and educational games are available to introduce the disciplines of academics through fun activities. CWMf feels that it is most important to reach kids at the earliest point in their developmental cycle.

Christopher Wallace Memorial Foundation
P.O. Box 834, Brooklyn, New York 11238
Tel. 718.399.0540/Tel. 570.629.1775 /Fax. 570.629.1088

Email: elisha.silvera@cwmfonline.org

Author Biography

Jake Brown resides in Nashville, Tennessee and is President of Versailles Records.

An avid writer, Jake has penned several books, including: *Suge Knight: The Rise, Fall and Rise of Death Row Records – The Story of Marion "Suge" Knight* and *YOUR BODY'S CALLING ME: Music, Love, Sex & Money—The Life & Times of "Robert" R. Kelly.* He is currently writing *The Unauthorized Biography of Fifty Cents… coming soon on Colossus Books.*

ORDER FORM

WWW.AMBERBOOKS.COM
African-American Self Help and Career Books

Fax Orders: 480-283-0991   Postal Orders: Send Checks & Money Orders to:
Telephone Orders: 480-460-1660   Amber Books Publishing
Online Orders: E-mail: Amberbks@aol.com   1334 E. Chandler Blvd., Suite 5-D67
                                                 Phoenix, AZ 85048

_____ *Ready to Die! The Life and Times of Biggie Smalls THE NOTORIOUS B.I.G.*
_____ *The African-American Writer's Guide to Successful Self-Publishing*
_____ *How to Be an Entrepreneur and Keep Your Sanity*
_____ *Fighting for Your Life*
_____ *The House that Jack Built*
_____ *Langhorn & Mary: A 19th American Century Love Story*
_____ *The African-American Woman's Guide to Great Sex, Happiness, & Marital Bliss*
_____ *The Afrocentric Bride: A Style Guide*
_____ *Beautiful Black Hair: A Step-by-Step Instructional Guide*
_____ *How to Get Rich When You Ain't Got Nothing*
_____ *The African-American Job Seeker's Guide to Successful Employment*
_____ *The African-American Travel Guide*
_____ *Suge Knight: The Rise, Fall, and Rise of Death Row Records*
_____ *The African-American Teenagers Guide to Personal Growth, Health, Safety, Sex and Survival*
_____ *Aaliyah—An R&B Princess in Words and Pictures*
_____ *Wake Up and Smell the Dollars! Whose Inner City is This Anyway?*
_____ *How to Own and Operate Your Home Day Care Business Successfully Without Going Nuts!*
_____ *The African-American Woman's Guide to Successful Make-up and Skin Care*
_____ *How to Play the Sports Recruiting Game and Get an Athletic Scholarship:*
_____ *Is Modeling for You? The Handbook and Guide for the Young Aspiring Black Model*

Name:_____

Company Name:_____

Address:_____

City:_____State:_____Zip:_____

Telephone: (____) _____E-mail:_____

For Bulk Rates Call: **480-460-1660**   ## ORDER NOW

Ready to Die! Biggie Smalls	$xxxxx	Sports Recruiting:	$12.95
Successful Self-Publishing	$14.95	Modeling:	$14.95
How to be an Entrepreneur	$14.95		
Fighting for Your Life	$14.95	❏ Check ❏ Money Order ❏ Cashiers Check	
The House That Jack Built	$16.95	❏ Credit Card: ❏ MC ❏ Visa ❏ Amex ❏ Discover	
Langhorn & Mary	$25.95		
Great Sex	$14.95	CC#_____	
The Afrocentric Bride	$16.95	Expiration Date:_____	
Beautiful Black Hair	$16.95	**Payable to:**	
How to Get Rich	$14.95	Amber Books	
Job Seeker's Guide	$14.95	1334 E. Chandler Blvd., Suite 5-D67	
Travel Guide	$14.95	Phoenix, AZ 85048	
Suge Knight	$21.95		
Teenagers Guide	$19.95	**Shipping:** $5.00 per book. Allow 7 days for delivery.	
Aaliyah	$10.95	**Sales Tax:** Add 7.05% to books shipped to Arizona addresses.	
Wake Up & Smell the Dollars	$18.95		
Home Day Care	$12.95	**Total enclosed: $**_____	
Successful Make-up	$14.95		

LaVergne, TN USA
28 July 2010
191252LV00004B/74/A